Returning Home

Inviting daughters back to the Father

JASMINE MORRIS

Copyright

2017 Jasmine Morris

ISBN-13: 978-0692963449
ISBN-10: 0692963448

Roadmap

Dedication

This book is dedicated to my mom and dad. To my parents, I honor you. Thank you for continuously praying for me. Thank you for chasing me down when I was in the world. Thank you for caring for me. Thank you for showing me the way, the truth, and the light. Nothing you prayed, did, or said to me was ever in vain. Thank you for gracing me as I write this book. I appreciate you for letting me walk into the calling God has for me and holding me accountable to it. Dad, Mom—this one is for you.

I love you.

Introduction

Home—in this book, home represents our Heavenly Father. Much like being in a physical home, in Him there is love, comfort, rest, grace, peace, and protection. Even though we belong with Him, sometimes in the midst of our journey with Him, we forget our *why*; we forget who God is. God is our ultimate source of fulfillment (Psalm 16:11), God is our refuge and strength (Psalm 46:1), and God is our Great Shepherd, always leading us along the best *path* (Psalm 23:1). Everything we need can be found in Him. For some us, the circumstances we've faced or the paths we've journeyed on have clouded our judgement of who He is. Some of us have lost trust in the One we proclaim, while others have strayed away. Some of us never let Him encounter us in the deepest places of our hearts.

Through this book, God wants to dive deep into those places. He wants to breathe life into them with His truth and love. He wants to reveal His nature to us and meet us in the midst of our questions, assumptions, and wanderings to bring us back to Him again.

"Set up road signs; put up guideposts. Mark well the path by which you came. Come back again, my virgin Israel; return to your towns here. How long will you wander, my wayward daughter? For the Lord will cause something new to happen—Israel will embrace her God"
(Jeremiah 31:21-22 NLT).

While writing this book, the Holy Spirit also revealed to me that there is an awakening happening for those who have held tightly to shame and defeat. Through reading this book, they will rise up and become more aware of their identity in Christ. Through God's truths, we will join with the members of heaven to align ourselves with the heavenly perspective to become exactly who we were born to be. For the daughters who have been distracted, God wants to pull you back on course. For those who feel it's too late to pursue God again, He's removing the shade of shame that has kept you hidden from even trying. And for those who have grown weary in your journey with the Lord, He desires to uplift and revive your heart with His truth. Where the enemy has planted seeds of deception, God desires to untangle and unravel each one with His truth and love.

In Jeremiah 31, God invites the northern Kingdom of Israel to turn back to Him. They lost their awe and wonder of their God, they forgot who they were, they drifted away from the truth they had known, and they turned to other gods that could not satisfy them. As I read through this story, God reminded me of my own journey with Him and how when I first got saved, I went astray and wandered away from Him. I wondered how many other Kingdom daughters also dealt with remaining with the Father after they get saved. I received a vision from the Lord of those who have surrendered to the Lord; they slowly pulled down their hands away from praise due to trials, doubt, frustration, pain, and so much more.

This ignited a fire in me to tell every daughter: it's time to come back home. I'm telling you, it's time to come back to the Father.

Because of what Jesus did on the cross, we are all welcome *home*—we all can have a relationship with God. I believe that many of us have accepted the invitation to a relationship with God. We've said our "yes" to living for God. We know the latest worship songs, know the truth about who God is, sit in our church services faithfully, etc. And all these things are worthy of praise—Hallelujah! But let's face it: for some of us, we're tired, we're wrapped up in the pain of our past, or we're silently running from the One who we proclaim. In this book, I believe God wants to draw us back to Himself. He wants to remind us that with every invitation comes a devotion to the One who sent it. He wants to lovingly remove every distraction, and draw us back to the place where we belong.

God has come to specifically meet with *you* inside of this book. He wants to revive, restore and renew His daughters with His love. The heartbeat of this book is for us to come back to the basics of who God is and invite others on the journey with us. No matter where we've been, no matter how long it's been, He desires each one of us to be with Him. Even if you've been on the journey with God for years, there's something new that God wants to stir in your heart, too. He yearns to have each daughter back in His presence, seeking Him in all things.

This book will get messy. I challenge you to carefully soak yourself in these truths. Together, we will unpack the basic truths of our Abba Father. If you are led, feel free to mark up this book with a pen and take notes. This is an opportunity to realign with heaven's agenda and to get back to the original place you belong. This is my prayer over you:

"God, I ask that You meet with each one of Your daughters. To those who are weary, refresh them; show them that You care deeply for them. To those with hardened hearts, open them up to who You are again. Lord, we want Your presence in our life again. Without You God, we are nothing. Arrange hearts to match Yours, Oh Lord. Take us deeper and help us heal in the places we've been wounded. Create a clean heart in us God, and renew a loyal spirit within us. Lead us, guide us, and show us the way. And on the way, remind us of Your nature and Your goodness. God, we ask You to bring us back

home again—back to You—the place where we belong. In Jesus' name I pray, Amen.

"For the time is coming when I will restore the fortunes of my people of Israel and Judah. I will bring them home to this land that I gave to their ancestors, and they will possess it again. I, the Lord have spoken!" (Jeremiah 30:3 NLT)

He's calling us! He's calling us back to the place where we belong—let's go Home.

CHAPTER ONE:

My Journey Home

"I knew you before I formed you in your mother's womb.
Before you were born I set you apart and appointed you as my
prophet to the nations" (Jeremiah 1:5 NLT).

I remember the day like it was yesterday. I stepped slowly and hesitantly into my apartment's leasing office. As I sat in the manager's office, I began to tremble with fear of the outcome I saw approaching. As I waited, I thought about how God could possibly rescue me from this moment, but He didn't. I thought to myself, *"why won't God stop this from happening?"* I felt stupid for stepping out in faith only to face one of the hardest moments in my life. This is when I began to doubt the truth about God. I knew the truth, but in this moment, I struggled to believe it. As I waited silently for the manager to file everything into his computer, I remembered all of the places I lived while being in Atlanta. I had moved in and out of many homes due to roommate changes or different circumstances, and I thought that this home would be different.

After a few brief moments, he gave me *the look*. The harsh reality of rejection settled within me.

I was being evicted. In that moment, I shrunk. I felt so small. I felt so embarrassed. My heart was crushed, and my faith was non-existent. I lost hope. I felt myself wanting to crawl into the hole of depression. I wanted to abandon the truth of God that I had held onto. I felt like a failure, and I was sure that God was overlooking me. I wanted to be home. I had moved to Atlanta in faith, and family was far away. I wanted to finally have something stable. After growing up in a broken home, hardship always seemed to be my story. *This* was just icing on the cake of what already seemed like a wasted life.

Here's a little backstory. I started building a web design business once I moved to Atlanta. It was great in the beginning. I was constantly booking clients and income was flowing. I wish the story ended pleasantly, but it didn't. Eventually, my clientele grew dry and so did my bank account. My finances began to spiral out of control. I was crazy behind on bills, and I had bill collectors calling me multiple times a day. I hit rock-bottom, both financially and spiritually.

I've learned that God is full of grace, and sometimes in His grace He has to pull us out of things that are not for us to protect us. For me, neither that apartment nor that business were for me. In fact, I started the business because I was running from my then retail management job that I hated and quit *prematurely*. So, I started this business from a place of frustration, not because God instructed me to. So, the Lord came in like a good Father and rescued me before I made a bigger mess.

After moving out of that apartment, I was graciously welcomed into a church family's home to stay. Moving in with them was probably the best decision I could have made. They walked me through that season and loved on me like I had *never* experienced before. It was right there in my mess when the grace of God came flooding in. While there, I was offered a newly-created position in the same mall that my old job was located in. I've learned that sometimes God takes you back around an old mountain to learn what you might've missed before. God definitely has a sense of humor. I stayed with church family until I got back on my feet.

Then, after fighting it, the Lord told me to move back in with my uncle. This move killed my pride, because I moved in with my uncle when I first moved to Atlanta in 2015. My uncle lives in a *quiet* country town far away from the city. Moving back in with him didn't make sense to me, but I obediently moved again.

What I didn't know is that throughout all the trials I faced in Atlanta, I had truly just forgotten who God was. I needed to be refreshed in His love and Word. All the financial troubles and disappointments cluttered how I saw Him and also how I saw myself. It was like I was starting over with the basics. When I opened up my hands from the *strong* grip I had on my life, He reintroduced me to His goodness. After pursuing His presence even more, I began to see that none of those homes mattered. It didn't matter if I didn't have a home to call my own and it didn't matter if I was just evicted, because for the first time ever I found out that *He was home.* He was my safe haven, He was my place of rest, and He was and is my hope.

I had to re-learn that God wasn't just a God who wanted me to bow down and serve Him, but He was a God who wanted to heal me from the inside out. He wanted to heal how I perceived Him. For me, I truly learned about who God is in the "wilderness seasons" of my life. After everything I had ever held onto was stripped away, my eyes were finally opened to Him. I learned that sometimes, He doesn't take you out of the wilderness when you desire escape. In His love, He kept me in the barren places so I could be confident in who He is and so that I could see that He is all that I need. He became the Promised Land I was searching for. Sometimes we seek out other things in hopes that they will fill us, but He is our hope, our strength, and our source.

So, I'm here to tell you that my story is a mess. You may think that yours is, too. And hey, we can meet here together. But before you committed that horrible sin, I probably did it first. Before you made that mistake, I probably stepped into it first. I'm the example, the picture of a messy life. But that's not the banner I wear—I now wear the banner of restoration, redemption, and freedom. I had to come into the knowledge of who God is on my own; when that truth finally hit me, it landed me on the mountaintop of freedom.

My Younger Days

Growing up, I wasn't your typical kid. I kept to myself most of the time and I was *super* shy. My smile wasn't the greatest. I had gaps all throughout my teeth and I was always the super-skinny girl in my class. I think that my shyness came from insecurity about my smile—I rarely desired interaction with other kids at school or even outside of school. Not only that, but I always felt like I was extremely behind in school. It was hard for me to learn the way other kids learned and, while I don't know for sure if I had a learning disability, I truly believe I did.

Even throughout middle school and high school, I would sit in class with sweaty palms, just completely filled with anxiety. About what, you ask? I was afraid of someone hearing my stomach growl. Now, before I go on, I want you to know that I was well-nourished at home, but for some odd reason, whenever I would get into the classroom, my stomach would grumble all over again. Can anybody relate? Those little things made me so nervous and embarrassed.

Speaking of embarrassment, remember those painful picture days you had to participate in each year in elementary school? I wish I could tell you in person how much I hated it, but this description will have to do for now. I remember that day, I was dressed in a brown dress with little pink flowers on it, ruffles at the top and bottom. Cute, I know. As I approached the line for the photography booth, I remember feeling an overwhelming sense of insecurity fall on me. In that moment, I felt overdressed and looked-down-upon by the other kids at school. I just remember feeling out-of-place and wanting to escape the cafeteria we were in.

Finally, it was my turn for a photo. I sat down on that hard photographer's stool, getting in position to have my photo taken. The photographer was adjusting the focus of the camera and making sure I was in alignment, then he asked me to smile. Now, remember, I didn't like to show my teeth because of all my gaps, so smiling was a huge deal to me. But I did it because I wanted to be like the rest of the kids and feel "normal." I put on the best smile I could, and one of the kids in line said out loud and in front of everyone, "Eww, her smile is retarded..."

I look back on this comment now and I laugh, but between you and me, I felt overcome with so much shame. I couldn't help but to feel defeated and less-than, just by those words alone. So, what did this do to me? It started me out on a trail of trying to live in a safe place where no one could ever hurt me. I was bullied with words in school, so to avoid getting hurt again, I avoided people in general; the pain of rejection was too much to bear. During this time, I know for a fact that the seed of rejection and shame was planted in my heart.

At an early age, my hope was found in whoever accepted me, but guys and promiscuity took the lead. Even though my mom brought my siblings and I to church, and I said the prayer of salvation at eleven years old, I didn't quite understand who God was to me. I wish I could tell that eleven-year-old version of myself that, though she feels alone, God is with her. It would have prevented so much pain, heartache, and misery. But I know that nothing is wasted with the Lord, so even though a lot of things happened to me as a child, I now get to share my freedom in Christ with others around me.

At eleven years old, I was introduced to pornography. I used to hang out with a group of girls in elementary school who were just as confused as I was. They had been in touch with their sexuality *well* before I was, and would slowly show me what they learned. Because I was already in a place of not understanding my worth and value and being a slave to people's opinions of me, I stepped into unknown territory. Whenever we had sleepovers, they would put on shows and porn videos and just watch them. It wasn't long before we wanted to try out the things we saw on the videos. As a young girl, my innocence was stripped, just like that. I did things with my classmates that drove me deeper into lust. This is exactly what the enemy wanted for my life—to be a slave to lust.

Lust was something that would follow me and continue to follow me until I broke up with it almost a *decade* later. It is a *nasty spirit* that drove me to places I never thought I'd see, doing things I never thought I'd do. After all, I grew up in a safe, well-provided-for military family. Looking at those types of things or doing those things wasn't something you would expect from me. But as times and seasons changed, my parents changed as well. The constant back-and-forth and fighting within their unstable marriage made me feel unwanted and unnoticed. I remember hearing the rage in my dad's voice some nights. I wanted to just run and hide. Even though he said with his mouth he loved me, I watched as he stood and completely belittled my mother. As a little girl, it broke my heart.

I couldn't do anything to help their failing marriage, so I believed the lie that I was the problem. I didn't think it was fair that I had to grow up in this type of family. In fact, I believe that is why I felt a sense of belonging when I was with those "friends." It wouldn't take long before my parents called it quits and divorced when we were stationed in Hawaii. Even though my siblings and I found such freedom boogie boarding on the waves and eating Spam Musubi, it was time to go back home. So, my mom decided to come back to Alabama, the place where her mother was. We went from a four-bedroom house to a small three-bedroom apartment, and at times my mom slept on the couch. My grandmother was sick and my mom was going through this difficult season of her life, so she decided it would be best to be around family.

At this point, I had created an entire world of watching porn. All the while, no one really knew about my secret life. Because I didn't know how to verbally communicate my pain, I found an escape that numbed the pain. Sure, my parents wanted the whole family in counseling, but all I did during those sessions was cry. So, porn ended up being my secret escape when things got hard, even at that age. I didn't realize it was going to cause such an addiction in my life until I got into high school in Alabama. Once I got there, I realized that there was a whole new realm of promiscuity that I wanted to explore. By this time, I had developed in my looks a little and I felt a bit more confident as braces had helped my smile. But even though I was blossoming,

I still had low self-esteem. So, now instead of trying to grab my computer screen, I wanted to grab the attention of guys. And it worked.

All my time was spent jumping in and out of new relationships. They never lasted longer than three or four months, but at least I had somebody, right? Looking back on it now, I really wanted love and attention from my dad, but I sought after it in these relationships. In high school, there was a real pressure to lose one's virginity. I'm pretty certain that most of my classmates had already tested the waters, and I truly felt like I was the only one who was still a virgin. One night, I gave up my virginity to someone who would share it with the whole school the very next day. Because it was already a small town, it wasn't long before the whole community knew. At this point, I knew I wanted our relationship to end.

When I ended that relationship, it only led me to another form of escape—partying and drinking. You might be thinking, *you partied and drank in high school?* Yes. Being around a certain circle of friends threw me into a lifestyle that was never created for me. Church was still something my mother clung to and she was always a praying woman (thank God for praying moms). Without her, I don't think I would have made it. She fervently prayed over all her kids, but especially me. I was known as the "rebellious child" during high school. I would cuss, lie, steal, and stay out really late on the weekends to be with my friends or the new guy I was currently "dating." If you knew me back then, you'd probably say that I needed to be in some sort of rehabilitation camp for girls. It was pretty bad. I had grown into this person that just didn't care; the truth is, I didn't think anyone truly cared about me, which is what I wanted all along.

College Days

This mindset carried me into college, into the night scene where I found myself falling in love with the lights, the crowds of people, and the loud music. It drove me so far away from the little bit of God that my mom tried to instill in me; it set me on the path of dysfunction and destruction. It drew me into the place where I was now that hypocrite Christian. Although I claimed Christianity, I certainly didn't live like it. In my eyes, attending church meant that I was "good with God," or somehow because my mom was deep in her faith, that's all it took. At this place in my life, I really didn't think that what I was doing was wrong.

The truth is, the deeper I fell into that lifestyle, the more bad things started to happen to me. And I knew it wasn't by chance that they were happening—they were signs that I needed to change. I just didn't want to change. So, there would continue to be a series of things that grabbed my attention: there was a shoot-out at the club I was at, my grades were failing, I lost my license and keys at a party, and I got terribly sick from consuming too much alcohol. It all started to take a toll on me. Eventually, I started praying every morning in my dorm's shower. There wasn't much to the prayer, but I do distinctly remember asking God to help me.

Although I woke up in the morning next to the guy I was dating, I still felt empty inside. Something in me yearned for more. Now, I see that it was God pulling on my heart to come into a relationship with Him, but at the time I didn't perceive it as that. One by one, I saw every relationship that I entered into fail. The closer graduation day approached, the more desperate I became for love. I guess it was the fear of me getting older, and still not having a beautiful love story that I had always wanted. Every guy that I met didn't want a seriously-committed relationship, and something about that made me furious. So, I took that frustration into what I didn't realize would be my last relationship before I surrendered.

In that last relationship, I bullied my boyfriend. If he showed me a glimpse of my exes, I would bring it up and start an argument. I was angry and I was hurting. If I can put words to my deepest heart's cry, it would say, "why won't you love me?!" That eleven-year-old Jasmine who was hurt, unnoticed, and unloved would resurface. The older Jasmine had to decide whether she would finally surrender or continue in dysfunction. Because my dad wasn't emotionally present as a child, my pain began to be illuminated and the wounds of my past were being exposed.

I went from a little girl wondering where I belonged, to being rejected by man, to seeing that no man could ever love me the way that I hoped to be. I came to a place where I was forced to confront my issues. Waking up the next day with a hangover and mascara smudged across my face was unfulfilling; I knew I didn't need a man to repair me. The search couldn't go on any longer; I needed something else and I wanted something else. I wanted another life. I needed a clean slate because the mess I had made in my life was too much for me to handle.

I decided to end the relationship. Since I was very mean to him, breaking it off was best for the both of us. This time, I didn't have another guy lined up to get into a relationship with. No. This time I wanted more. I wanted something to fill me. I wanted the deepest desire in my heart to be fulfilled. But going to church wasn't an option. If I was going to establish a relationship with the Lord, then I had to discover Him on my own and in my own way.

Christmas week of December of 2013, everything changed. During this time, God met with me. I was on Christmas break at my dad's place, and I was reading through my Facebook timeline when I discovered my sister had re-posted a post from a woman named Heather Lindsey. I noticed she was happily-married, she loved the Lord, and she was beautiful. I couldn't help but to be drawn to her life, her family, and eventually I stumbled upon her story.

I put down my phone when I saw this, and I grabbed my laptop to get a better view of her blog, heatherllindsey.com. Because there wasn't a quiet place in my dad's apartment, I went to the bathroom. I ignored everything else in that moment because all I wanted to do was read more of her story.

What I didn't realize is that when I walked into that bathroom, I was walking into an altar time, uniquely-designed just for me and my Father. I opened up my laptop and began to briefly scan through the words she wrote. It seemed as if the words were jumping off the page at me and landing so sweetly upon my heart. I was introduced to a warm feeling I hadn't known before. As I began to weep, everything that I had been searching for my entire life became so clear to me. It became so evident that I chose to live this chaotic life, but I no longer had to. I wanted to and I *needed* to live for the God she worshipped. He was the answer I was looking for.

I placed my laptop aside, got down on my knees and I began to cry out to God. It was the most imperfect prayer filled with tears. Somehow I knew that God would understand me. I just wanted

God to know that I was sorry about how I was living, but before I could even carry on anymore, He knew. His presence hovered over me like a thick cloud. I wept for nearly an entire hour because everything in my life finally made sense. It was like, "Aha! THIS is why I have been feeling so broken."

I chased after so many things that left me feeling empty, but that night I found who I was supposed to chase. I chased Him with my entire heart, and I longed for Him more and more.

To say that my moment of salvation was perfect would be a lie. In fact, it was a complete mess. But God knew about my mess even before I even knew there was one. God lovingly pulled me out of the mud and gave me the clean start I so desired.

I put on His robe of righteousness and I pursued to know Him more by buying my first Bible, which I still have today. God led me to resources, studies, and sermons online that I could learn from. One of those resources was the Gathering Oasis Church. I would listen to their podcasts and sermons online. He placed people in my life to lead me on the right path and lead me closer to Him. Although my journey with Him wasn't perfect, He led me to a life of purpose and an identity that I had desperately longed for.

He set me up to meet people I never knew I would meet, and took me places I never thought I would go. He especially knew I needed to move out of my home in Alabama, so He moved me to Atlanta, GA. Moving to Atlanta birthed something that I didn't realize was in me—leading worship. Singing was one of the things I had left on the shelf once I began to chase after meaningless things, but God, in His grace, saw fit to allow me to pick it back up again. Even though I was perfectly fine with lifting my hands in the congregation, the Lord led me to a *very* special woman who saw that gift of leading worship inside of me. She not only taught me how to lead worship, but she also pushed me further towards Christ unlike ever before. Although I wanted to stay in the background, the Lord brought me up a little further. Today, I lead worship at the Gathering Oasis Church; the same church Heather Lindsey and her husband planted. God is amazing, right?

All that I needed was right in front of me. He set up road signs so that I knew how to return back to Him. He intentionally designed specific circumstances to happen so that I had the opportunity to choose Him. There's no way that I would be who I am today without God; in fact, I am nothing without God. Today, I am so full of the life God has given me. He has made *all things* new and I am certain that if God did it for me, He can do it for you too.

When it seemed like I had nowhere to go, when it seemed like I didn't belong, God brought me home. He brought me back to the place where I belonged. I share this with you in hopes to encourage you that no matter what your family was like, how you were brought up, or what your grades looked like in school—God can truly make all things new in your life. You may question if you will ever live beyond the life you have lived. But before you had questions, God had answers. He mapped out a beautiful redemption plan in advance for you. His plans are good. His goodness and grace doesn't just apply to me, it applies to you as well. You are a living, breathing creation that God blew His life into and declared "good." He's invested in you. Whether you've been saved for a little while or a long time, know this: nothing you have done in your past will ever discount you from what God has for you. Nothing.

If you find yourself reading this book and you have yet to give your life to Christ, know this: *If you confess your sins to God, He is faithful and just to forgive you of your sins and to cleanse you from all wickedness* (1 John 1:9 NLT). God isn't looking for a perfect yes, He just needs your yes. He desires for you to live in close fellowship with Him. His love will compel you to turn from the ways of this world.

Because of the Cross, you can have freedom; because of the cross, you can come Home.

During my journey to God, I learned this important truth: God's nature *never* changes (Malachi 3:6). He will never stop being faithful. He will never stop being kind. He will never stop being just. You can run across the longest valley, sink into the deepest ocean, or climb the highest mountain, and never escape His love (Psalm 139). His mercy knows no end and His love for you is beyond anything you've ever seen. When you trust Him, I believe that God will do exceedingly and abundantly more than you could ever ask or think in your life (Ephesians 3:20).

I struggled to trust Him. In fact, the journey to God only began that night in the bathroom. That night gave route to a continuous pursuit of Him and His presence. It seemed scary at first, but as I began to learn to trust the One leading me, I found that the trail that He left for me began to look more like the path that I was searching for all along. As I embarked on the journey, He led me on an adventure to know Him more and to become more like His son. And so, I journeyed on...

"Therefore, if anyone is in Christ, the new creation has come; the old has gone, the new is here!" (2 Corinthians 5:17)

CHAPTER TWO:

Home

As I mentioned at the beginning of this book, the word *Home* represents our Heavenly Father. With the word *Home* representing our Abba Father, it's important that we have a clear picture of who He really is. Within this chapter, I want to focus in on who God is to *you.* Have you ever meditated on who God is? What do you think about when you think of Him? Being that we are all at different places in our walks with Him, your response may be different than mine, and that's okay. It is okay if we are at different stages in our relationship with Him. We're all learning and growing at different paces; however, we must lay down some very important foundational truths about God's nature. The knowledge of these beautiful truths, along with the truths in His Word, will be the solid foundation for our growth in Him.

This chapter is important because I believe most of us lose sight of these basic truths throughout our Christian faith. So as simplistic as these truths may seem, I challenge you to lean into each one of them and apply them to your everyday life. I've seen how many believers struggle with these truths when faced with a new test or trial. I believe that sometimes we can have *so much* head knowledge about God that we never let the truths penetrate *our hearts*. This only lands us on a plateau, leaving us unable to lead others into an authentic relationship with God. Leading from a place of intimacy with God is the aim; if we've never encountered Him for ourselves, yet we're filled with head knowledge, we can't lead others where we've never truly been. I wonder what would happen if we took the time to really meditate on these truths. I wonder how much pain, worry, and dysfunction we could avoid if we would establish ourselves in His Word. I truly believe that you will begin to flourish in your walk with the Lord as you meditate on these stunning truths and let His Spirit lead you *in all things*.

Because of what Jesus Christ did on the cross, we can come freely and boldly to God's throne of grace (Hebrews 4:16). This means that we can have access to a relationship with God because of the blood that Jesus shed on the cross. *Anyone* who confesses their sins and believes that Jesus is Lord can have access to a relationship with Him (1 John

1:9). Not only do we have access to a relationship with Him, but we also have permission to sit at His feet and study His nature.

It is *good* to want to know Him more; in fact, He wants us to be fully aware of who He is. I say this because often times, even after we get saved, questions arise about who He is and we hesitate to address them. We don't want to seem faithless or ignorant to the truth of God. But we have no reason to fear because we have been purchased by the blood of the Lamb. We are His! He understands our questions, doubts, and concerns. He wants to reassure us in His Word about His nature. It is not that we are to remain in our questions and doubts, but it is ok to be real, raw, and uncut with God. It helps our faith to grow.

Take a seat and pull out your pen as we refresh ourselves in the Word. I want to encourage you to study God's word on your own time as well—it will help you tremendously in your walk. I want to give you a few simple truths about our gracious Heavenly Father.

Three Basic Truths About God

1) True satisfaction can only be found in Him

"You make known to me the path of life; in your presence,
there is fullness of joy; at your right hand are pleasures
forevermore"
(Psalms 16:11 ESV).

God can fulfill *every* part of our being. He
actually created us to only be whole in Him
(Colossians 2:10). He makes known to us the path of
life. This means that there is another path that leads
to death. But how beautiful is it that He wants to
show us the way of *life?* When we're in His presence,
He fills *every void* with His love and truth. He
contains everything that we were designed to enjoy.
We also find satisfaction in the evidence of His
glory: our friends that laugh with us, our family that
cares for us, the cool breeze on a summer day, the
bristling trees in our backyard, the sunset on the
horizon, the crunchy bite of an apple, the exciting
aroma of coffee, and the deliciousness that is ice

cream. All of these things were created for us to enjoy!

We get to enjoy His creation within the safe parameters that He has graciously set for us. Even during the times when you feel lonely and it's hard for you to truly enjoy the work of His hands, He's there for you. Even when you're not basking in the laughter of friends or the care of your family, He's there for you. When you need a friend, He is a friend to the lonely (John 15:15). He gives us the courage to face hard things and leads us through painful things (Isaiah 41:10). He has a nurturing spirit that fills us with a fatherly love that each one of us longs for (Psalm 68:5). Whether you're needing the company of a friend or dealing with a broken heart, I dare you to try Him. Whatever you're in need of can be found in Christ.

2) *He is a good Father*

"Even if my father and mother abandon me, the Lord will hold me close" (Psalms 27:10 NLT).

When I needed a dad the most, God showed me He was one. I have always had an earthly father in my life, but my deepest longing was to have a father who was not just there physically, but also emotionally. My dad said he loved me with his lips, but it always felt like a fight to have his heart. As a little girl, I *craved* that from my dad. The hunger only *grew* once I got older. Thankfully, I now know that God is a Father to me, and this truth has truly changed me *forever*. I learned that our Heavenly Father isn't harsh; He is kind. He corrects in love and He loves *unconditionally*. He is the exact opposite of what I witnessed growing up and it drew me even closer to Him. Maybe the love you received wasn't the best growing up, or maybe you've never seen God as your Father. I would encourage you to taste and see that the Lord is good. He is a good and perfect Father who shows us perfect love. He is eagerly waiting for His daughters to recognize it.

For many of us, it will take re-learning what a good father is supposed to look like. The Lord desires to uproot any misconceptions you've had of a father and lead you into His truth. I ask that you open up your heart as we dive into these truths about our Abba Father. *Declare this over yourself:*

My Father's love is *perfect* (1 John 4:18). His *love* for me knows no end (Jeremiah 31:3). He is a Father whose love *chases* me down even when I try to run away (Psalm 139). He is a Father who doesn't miss *anything* about my life (Psalm 139:17-18; Isaiah 49:15; Jeremiah 29:11). He is a Father who has me *memorized* (Luke 12:7). He has promises for me (Jeremiah 1:5, Psalm 12:6). He is a Father who wants me to be brave and courageous (Joshua 1:9). He is a Father of second chances (Jonah 1-3, Romans 4:7). He is a Father who understands my weaknesses and burdens (Matthew 11:30, Psalm 34:18). He is a Father who is jealous for me (Deuteronomy 4:24). He is a Father who illuminates the path for me (Psalm 32:8). He provides my every need (Philippians 4:19). He always has good plans for me (Jeremiah 29:11).

Over two thousand years ago, God showed His great love for you by sending His Son to die on the cross. He has been patiently waiting as you come into the knowledge of Him as your Father. He longs for you to know Him as that (Jeremiah 3:19). Ever since Jesus died and rose from the grave, God has been longing for us to know Him as our Father. He created *you*. He thought about you before anyone else did, and He was your heavenly Father long before you even had an earthly one. He loves you more than you know. I encourage you to embrace Him as your Heavenly Father; seeing Him in this way will truly transform your walk with Him.

3) God is faithful.

One of the biggest ways we as daughters begin to pull back in our relationship with God is by not reflecting on His faithfulness. *"Is He trustworthy? Is depending on Him really worth it?"* many of us may ask. The biggest way to combat any fear or any doubt that God isn't faithful is by knowing that God's nature doesn't change. He is steadfast. He is constant even when we are not. He's always there, waiting for us to come into the realization of His unchanging nature.

"Jesus Christ is the same yesterday, today and forever"
(Hebrews 13:8 NLT).

Having trouble trusting God? Look back and study His nature through His Word and your own journey with Him. When has He ever failed you? Ask Him to reveal moments when He was faithful. He will show you. Let that be your hope when worry, doubt, and fear arise. The Lord spoke this revelation to me a few months ago and I thought I would share it with you:

"If you keep your eyes fixed on His nature, you'll never question the journey."

That's the truth. Our paths will change and our situations will change, but if we place our gaze on the One who has the *purest intentions* for us, we won't question the journey.

Even the words that He speaks will never return empty. It is in His nature to speak and fulfill—*every single time.* He doesn't speak without fulfilling, and He doesn't move without following through:

"God is not a man, so he does not lie. He is not human, so he does not change his mind. Has he ever spoken and failed to act? Has he ever promised and not carried it through?"
(Numbers 23:19 NLT)

We can sing a lot of songs about God's faithfulness, or hear about it through sermons, but the reality is that we must *know* for ourselves. It may take time, and it may even take a few hard seasons to actually know. But when you know—oh how it changes everything! Sisters, I invite you to pray into God's faithfulness. Declare it over yourself, even if you feel like your faith is weak. The more you say it and live it out, the more you'll begin to believe it. The road to knowing God's faithfulness is sometimes messy. You may have ups and downs, but you get back up to trust again. Throughout life, God undoes your fears, questions, and doubts until you collide with the truth that He is good, and He is so, so *faithful*.

"For my people will serve the Lord their God and their king descended from David—the king I will raise up for them" (Jeremiah 30:9 NLT).

CHAPTER THREE:

The Journey to Intimacy

Jesus died on the cross to bridge the gap between God and man that sin created. Because of His sacrifice, our sins are covered and we can live in unity with God. The Father's love drove Jesus to earth to bring His sons and daughters Home. He has invited each one of us into a loving relationship with Him; no matter our age, race, background, or mistakes, He wants each one of us. While we are invited into a relationship with God, it is truly up to us to decide how close we get to Him. The Bible says that if we draw near to God, He will draw near to us (James 4:8). While He is always pursuing us, we have to do our part by stepping closer to Him. A relationship of any kind takes effort on *both ends*, and our relationship with God is no different. He loves us, so He gave us free will. He will oftentimes wait patiently *for us* to respond to His pursuit. No matter how you came to know God, He wants to be so, so close to you. He wants you to tell Him your deepest secrets, how you like to wear your hair, your fears, and so much more.

I believe that throughout this chapter, God wants to show you *how to* get closer to Him. It's one thing to give your heart to Christ, but your relationship is taken to another level when you *choose* to know Him more. Maybe you've been asking and seeking Him on how to go deeper, but you never really knew the steps to take to do so. My hope and prayer is that you'd find practical steps to grow intimately in your relationship with the Lord—that it would be vibrant again and flourish beyond your wildest imaginations. Let's journey home, shall we?

"You will seek me and find me when you seek me with all your heart" (Jeremiah 29:13 NIV).

Highest Priority

Things that we value, we prioritize. We map out time for valuable things and people. In order to know God on a deeper level or Him at all, we must place Him as the highest priority in our lives. Nothing can take His place; absolutely nothing. I want you to know that I tried to place God last, second, and sort-of-first in past seasons. I wanted to know God more, but I was still holding on to my "me time" and other distractions. Now, let me clarify—there's nothing wrong with having alone time, but I began to separate my God time from my alone time, instead of allowing God into my alone time. It was like when I was having "my time," I was focused on my phone, my laptop, vlogs on YouTube, and I didn't worry about anything else. I switched gears in these moments and my phone became my hope and source of fulfillment. There's a difference between being entertained by technology and being addicted to the fulfillment or lack thereof that it brings. My question for you is this: *If it was His priority to save us, shouldn't it be our highest priority to pursue Him?*

So, how do you balance your relationship with God with everyday life? I have found that we actually make this a lot more complicated than it really is. It's quite simple: we are to seek Him in all things. *In all your ways acknowledge Him, and He shall direct your paths* (Proverbs 3:6 NKJV). There's no formula to this. Each one of our relationships with Him will look different, but He just wants us to seek Him in *all* things. This means, before you apply to that school or before you get into that relationship, He wants to be a part of it. Have you ever met that dad who sits on the front row of a game and literally watches their son or daughter's every step? God's that Dad. He wants to be a part our everyday lives.

Intimacy

Intimacy: a close, familiar, and usually affectionate or loving personal relationship with another person or group.

I look back on the story of Abraham and how he developed a super close relationship with God. God told Him secrets (Genesis 18:20-21). Isn't that the coolest thing ever? God, the Creator of Heaven and Earth sharing His secrets? Amazing! On the contrary, we see Abraham's family living in Sodom and Gomorrah, a city filled with sin. Abraham prayed to the Lord, waited on the Lord, and trusted the Lord. We learn from Abraham's example that communication is key to building an intimate relationship with God. We must seek Him in prayer; that is how we get to learn His heart. Prayer is the driving force that grows our intimacy with Him. Not only that, but vulnerability in our prayers will also help us to know God more and trust Him.

My relationship with God completely changed when I became open with God about my feelings. I started to see that He was a safe place to cry out and be myself with when the world around me misunderstood me. Prayer is one way we get to know Him, but the Word He gave us carries us even deeper. The Bible is life-giving! We can capture pieces of God's heart through the words we read. This builds an unbreakable intimacy, because once you know He is for you, you will want to keep coming back. When you know He loves you, you just want more of Him. When you know He will *always* be there for you, you'll never want to leave.

Have you ever met a married couple that sort of look like each other? Or maybe they do or say the same thing at the exact same time? This is what intimacy looks like; they've grown to know each other and because of that, they can be on the same page. It is the same way with God. He wants to be so extremely close to you that you begin to say or do the same things He would. He wants you to be so in tune with Him that His very nature reflects off of you. We should hunger for this place of closeness, even with our greatest falls, flaws, and our many imperfections. He doesn't need you to be perfect, He just needs your "yes."

Hearing His Voice

Do you know that God speaks to you? Maybe you've never heard Him speak before, but He always is. He speaks through people, songs, and His Word. But we should never limit *how* God will speak; after all, He is God and He can use anything and anyone. We should never be afraid that we don't hear from God, because He speaks to each one of us differently. For one person, He may use a word from a person to deliver a message to them. This person connects to the message and recognizes that God is speaking directly to them. We can see an example of this in Jeremiah chapter 26, where Jeremiah spoke over God's people. The prophet Jeremiah spoke a word over the people that came straight from the mouth of God. The people were able to hear from God through this willing vessel. Maybe you're thinking, "yeah, I know God spoke through Jeremiah, Moses, and all these other Bible people, but I want to hear God speak to *me*." Or perhaps you've heard God's voice, but it's cluttered by other confusing, negative voices.

I want to break this down for you as simply as I can: **He can speak to you directly.** He speaks to me directly, and I know this because there is peace attached to this voice. I hear it and I know it's not me.

It catches my attention by how gentle and peaceful it is. I've met other Christians who hear from God in a different way. They may walk into a room and discern a certain spirit, or what God is doing in that moment. They just *know*. I've also met others who have visions and dreams and this is how God speaks to them. They will have a dream and instantly know what God is doing in their hearts, in the lives of those around them, in their nation, in the world, or in the spirit realm. I first encountered hearing the voice of God after watching a sermon. A pastor was talking about how it took him years to hear the voice of God. He shared how it took him seeking God consistently in his prayer closet, just waiting on Him to speak. After this sermon, I was so inspired to hear from God. I had just cut off a toxic relationship, so I became *desperate* to hear God's voice. I believe God waited to see how serious I was about Him and hearing His voice, so He waited until that moment, after that sermon, to speak to me. He said this:

My journal entry – February 2, 2015

"Boy, I did not expect Him to speak the way He did. He told me that my trust in Him will carry me from season to season…and Lord-willing, into a relationship. He showed me that my faith will transfer. He also showed me that there are deeper issues in my heart that would affect my relationships and because He wants me in relationships with people, He's showing me how to overcome these issues."

There are a few things I want to remind you of when it comes to hearing God's voice. Here they are: *The voice of God will always be in alignment with the Word of God. It will never be negative, belittling, or discouraging. It will always teach and not condemn. It will never pull you away from God; it will always push you closer to Him.*

Transparency

Prior to learning about intimacy, it was so hard for me to be vulnerable with the Lord, likely because of the damage that took place in my life. I was hurting. I built a wall around my heart, trying to guard Him from coming completely in. This was my safe place, or so I thought it was. Once I agreed to go deeper with Him, He blew every hard shell away as if it were as light as a feather. I began to see that transparency was necessary. I began to see that my lack of transparency hindered my growth with the Lord. I learned that He didn't want the, "Oh God, You're so holy…" type of prayers, but He just wanted me to share with Him whatever was on my heart. He loves honesty. This reminds me of David—his prayers to the Lord were real and raw:

"Bend down, O Lord, and hear my prayer; answer me, for I need your help. Protect me, for I am devoted to you. Save me, for I serve you and trust you. You are my God."
(Psalm 86:1-2 NLT).

"For I need your help," David said. David wasn't afraid to admit that he was weak in this moment. I can't imagine the closeness that was developed after the Lord helped him. This probably shifted the way David viewed God. This is what happens when we open ourselves up to God, too. We begin to view Him totally different than we did before. It gives us a new, fresh perspective on our relationship with the Lord. No longer is He just a God we pray to, but now He's our God that knows and holds our hearts, yet still loves us the same.

Consistency

We grow intimately with God by consistently entering into His presence. It is the most powerful way we can develop intimacy with the Lord. I often hear women say, "ugh, I missed my quiet time today..." and I want you to know that it's okay. God isn't mad at you when you don't spend time with Him, so don't beat yourself up. We should never create a law out of intimacy with Him, but what we must strive to keep getting back up. It's important that we participate in consistency by laying aside every weight that slows us down. These weights could be our phones, television, sleep, food, or anything else. I say food, because at one point, I had to realize that the foods I was eating, (especially my late-night smorgasbord filled with heavy to-go Asian food and super-sweet Kettle Corn) was not good for my health. Not only was it not good for my health, but it was also a weight that was slowing me down from pursuing God. I had no energy! The food was sucking up all of my energy.

What are your weights? What are you carrying that is slowing you down from entering into closeness with Him? **There's a price that comes with being close to Him, are you willing to pay it?** And in a world filled with tons of distractions, as believers, we must strip off even more weights than we might think. It might take you waking up at 5 a.m. every morning, or staying up later. No matter the time He tells you, be obedient and remain consistent. The constant coming back to Him builds an unbreakable foundation of intimacy with the Lord. We should seek to build this type of intimacy with the Lord before anyone else. If we can steward consistency in our pursuit of Him, we will *flourish* in our relationship like never before.

"...*You have been chosen to know me, believe in me, and understand that I alone am God. There is no other God— there never has been, and there never will be*"
(Isaiah 43:10 NLT).

CHAPTER FOUR:

Roadblocks

When we're on our journey with Christ, there can oftentimes be distractions that get in the way of our pursuit of Him. I call these distractions *roadblocks*. These roadblocks are the sin in our lives; addictions, partying, sex outside of marriage, lying, cheating, gossiping, hoarding offense, worrying, and more. Ultimately, these roadblocks and **many** others can prevent us from growing closer to God and bringing others close to Him as well.

"It's your sins that have cut you off from God. Because of your sins, he has turned away and will not listen anymore" (Isaiah 59:2 NLT).

For many of us, we know who God is and we know what it looks like to live for Him. But unfortunately, the temptation of this world stands knocking at our door. I want you to know that the temptation you are facing is someone else's struggle, too. We all have roadblocks we have to push aside daily, but through Jesus Christ, we can overcome. The Word says:

"The temptations in your life are no different from what others experience. And God is faithful. He will not allow the temptation to be more than you can stand. When you are tempted, he will show you a way out so that you can endure"
(1 Corinthians 10:13 NLT).

These roadblocks are like broken cisterns. Cisterns are hollow, spacious places where you can store water. In the Middle East, cisterns were used for holding liquids, like rainwater. Throughout the Bible, God compares the sin of man to *cracked cisterns*.

"For my people have done two evil things: They have abandoned me—the fountain of living water. And they have dug for themselves cracked cisterns that can hold no water at all!" (Jeremiah 2:13 NLT)

We see here in scripture that God represents the fountain of living water. This means that our salvation, our hope, and our satisfaction comes from the Lord and Him alone. He is our source. Nothing else in this world can promise us *complete* satisfaction like the Lord does. No job, no man, no financial status—nothing! We can see that only God satisfies us in Isaiah 55:1-6. He must be our cistern because He never has and never will run dry. In John chapter four, there is a story told of a Samaritan woman traveling to a well. When she arrives, she meets face-to-face with the *living water*—Jesus Christ. He teaches her about salvation and invites her to live for Him despite her current promiscuous lifestyle. Although she hoped to receive drinking water, that day she encountered salvation.

Each one of us is to drink from the *living water*—our intimate relationship with Jesus Christ. However, many of us have found ourselves drinking from cracked cisterns, only to be left feeling ashamed and dissatisfied. When we pursue cracked cisterns, it breaks God's heart. It's almost as if He's saying, *"in Me you have everything you need, why are you searching in all the wrong places?"* I want you to know, I searched in all the wrong places, too. It was draining because I longed for something that would last, but nothing lasted. I journeyed to many cisterns throughout life, and every single one of them was dry and barren. Each one of them looked different. My ex was a broken cistern, my addition to porn was a broken cistern, and drinking alcohol was a broken cistern. Each cistern drained life out of me instead of pouring life into me, and I didn't even recognize it was until I hit rock-bottom. That's sort of what a broken cistern does—it makes you think from afar that it will satisfy you, but by the time you're done, you feel drained and ashamed.

I have found that when I am honest about my roadblocks, *God meets me where I am and showers me with His grace.* Not only that, but He gives me strategy to push aside what is blocking my path to Him. I want you to know that there's always grace available for you. Even those who have found themselves in the mud will be showered down with His grace. It might get messy in the honesty, but it is better to be honest than to keep it hidden. In the next few chapters, we're going to travel down some bumpy roads and align ourselves as daughters. We will no longer hide or run from the process God has us on. We will overcome every obstacle that hinders us from giving ourselves fully to God. I pray that through these words you will find hope and a newfound freedom in Christ.

"Rise up from the dust, O Jerusalem. Sit in a place of honor. Remove the chains of slavery from your neck; O captive daughter of Zion" (Isaiah 52:2 NLT).

CHAPTER FIVE

The Roadblock of Assumption

Assumptions—they are usually the leading roadblock that can hinder us from growing closer to the Lord. Maybe we assume God is not on our side, or that the situation that we're in won't work out for our good. Of course, we know that all things work out for our good, but sometimes our assumptions conclude that they won't. No matter the assumption, we can hinder our intimacy with the One that wants our hearts and trust most. It causes us to question day in and day out our Creator and places stress and worry on us that never belonged to us. Throughout this chapter, I hope to set up a road map that will allow you to see what is hindering your trust in the Lord. I'll teach you ways to move past those assumptions when they arise. Again, I believe this is so important that we address this because it is the number-one roadblock I believe most Christian women deal with today. Most desire to trust Him, but don't know where to begin.

I want to start out by saying that not all of your doubt will suddenly disappear within this chapter. I believe that with time and experience with the Lord, you will learn how to trust God. As you are learning, I pray you come back to these truths to draw you back to the path of complete dependency on your Abba Father.

Growing up, your parents may have said, "maybe," or "not right now" when you were asking permission for something. Maybe it was to hang out with friends, buy something, or if you were like me, to have more food after dinner. For some of us, it was really hard hearing "maybe." I'll admit it was difficult for me too; now that I'm older, I'm very thankful for my parents' maybes and definitely thankful for their nos. Our reaction to these responses may have left us feeling like they don't really want the best for us—especially if we *really* wanted it.

A lot of times, the way we react to God is the same way we reacted to our parents—upset and disappointed. We don't understand. We assume that He doesn't want what's best for us or that He's withholding good things from us. But God is the **perfect** Father; there is no flaw in Him. He knows exactly what we need, when we need it. He shows us the perfect time for everything and we never have to worry about Him forgetting about us. While our earthy parents may have fallen short, God never has and never will.

When your hope is in the One that doesn't change, you can always assume the best.

When God says *"no,"* or *"not right now,"* what is your response? Do you quickly assume He isn't going to give you His best, or do you assume that He's for you and has it under control? We can't assume that just because God said "wait" right now, that He means "no;" or just because it's not time right now, it means that it will never be time. He knows exactly what's best for us. I remember thinking at one point a friend of mine was so upset with me. She wasn't speaking to me, and I just felt out-of-the-loop in her life. But then, we ended up talking. It turned out that she was just in a really busy season, super stressed out and needed prayer. If I never would have spoken to her, I would have never known that she wasn't upset with me and life was crazy for her at the time. Do you see how one quick assumption can lead straight towards a false conclusion? This is what assumption does to us; it leads us into a place of doubt and insecurity. It also leads to conclusions birthed by fear and worry.

I wonder, how many times do we assume certain things about God and our season because we're not consistently communicating with Him? Communication kills assumptions, so in our case, prayer kills assumptions. When we pray, we are able to remain connected to the Father in such a way that we begin to understand His heart for us. It leaves no room for doubt, questions, or insecurities because *we know* what our Heavenly Father says about us. It's the same way with the reading of the Word and remaining in worship—they all destroy the lies, deception and assumptions all in one moment.

"Trust in the Lord with all your heart; do not depend on your own understanding" (Proverbs 3:5 NLT).

It's imperative that you receive what this scripture is saying. It says two things: one—trust in the Lord; two—do not depend on your understanding. A lot of times what we attempt to do is depend on our own understanding first and *then* try to trust the Lord, but it just doesn't work that way. If we *first* put our trust in the Lord, then there's nothing else to believe in, trust in, or depend on. We just believe His truth and nothing else. That is God's heart for you—that you would never lean on what you think is happening in your life, even if you feel like you're right. If you deal with assumptions and overthinking, I want you to know that these types of truths will wash away any worry or doubt. Stand on these truths even if your lights are being cut off, even if you can't go to college this year, and even if you find yourself single again.

Here's a beautiful example of this verse applied practically: My best friend once told me that in order to ease her worries, she just stops thinking about her problems after she prays about them. She doesn't neglect what's going on, but she lives as if it's already taken care of, because it already is. The Word tells us to cast our cares (this includes assumptions) unto the Lord (1 Peter 5:7) for

He cares for us. When assumptions *do* come up, run to Him with all your fears and He'll comfort you with His love and peace. Choose to not think about what could go wrong and begin thinking about the Lord's promises for you. When you meditate on God's truth, you can defeat lies. You are able to trade in your mindset for the mind of Christ; the mind of Christ doesn't fear, isn't shaken, and is un-moveable in every situation. We have the same power to throw off worry and fear and think on things that are pure and worthy of praise (Philippians 4:8). The truth is that 99.9% of the time, our worst fears and our what-ifs never happen.

Sometimes, assumptions can sneak in our lives in the tiniest ways. Maybe you're on your job and your boss calls you into the office. You assume that this is the moment you're about to lose your job even though she really just wanted to tell you how great of a job you're doing. We can destroy these assumptions by casting down imaginations that run rampant in our minds. The Bible even teaches us to cast down vain (empty, void, worthless) imaginations. So, if you begin to imagine something contrary to God's Word, you have the authority to cast it down with the Word of God (2 Corinthians 10:5 KJV).

Don't allow what you think to rule over your life. I've seen how it causes daughters to live in fear their entire lives, and God never intended them to live that way. We are to walk by faith and not by sight, or by our assumptions, no matter what season we may find ourselves in.

You might be thinking, "I know I overthink and I know I assume, but I just can't seem to break this constant cycle of going back and forth with trusting God." It seems like you're stuck and you want to break free. First, I want you to know that this faith walk is not a sprint, but a marathon. You learn how to trust God at your own pace. No one has it perfected; I know I don't. We are all learning and re-learning how to trust Him and that's okay. Every step you take brings you closer to Home.

"For God has not given us a spirit of fear and timidity, but of power, love, and self-discipline" (2 Timothy 2:7 NLT).

CHAPTER SIX:

Walking by Faith

Our journey with the Lord is a journey of *faith*, and sometimes in the midst of pursuing His plans for us, our faith is shaken. My prayer is that you would be strengthened and filled with faith by the end of this book. I want to mention some real battles that we often face and how to overcome them. If you don't deal with the root, you'll constantly circle back around the same issue. After you've identified the issue, you must then uproot it. After you dig up the roots, you can replace it with truth so that you can walk in joy, peace, and freedom. As we're going over these points, I encourage you to think about your own root issues and decide that you are going to replace those areas of doubt with faith. We must first begin with the root of our distrust. Here are some of the root issues of our distrust.

Betrayal: Often times, we don't fully trust God because people in our lives have hurt us, lied to us, or gotten over on us. This pain can cause us to be very hesitant about where we place our trust. But this is what we must remember about being hurt by people: they are flawed pieces of dust that we cannot depend upon. God being just, faithful, omnipotent, and perfect, we can depend upon Him. God is not like a human. He cannot lie and His love does not change. So, when you're tempted to believe that trusting in God isn't worth the risk, look back on His love, nature and character. You will begin to see who He truly is and you will begin to see people from the right perspective.

Trusting in what you can see vs. the Word of God: This past year, I visited my mom in Ohio. I sat in the very last seat on the plane. This was the seat with no window and it was right in front of the restroom. Yeah, I got really lucky that day. I remember thinking, "gosh, I wish I had a window seat." I'm still a little afraid of flying by myself, so I like to see what's going on in case things get "out of control." Whenever we hit turbulence, I felt like I was about to die and meet Jesus. I imagined that we were going to land in the ocean and I was going to wash up on shore like the movie Cast Away, stranded on a random island trying to find food in trees for survival. Much of our journeys with the Lord is like having a windowless seat on the plane.

You can't see what's going on, but He just requires you to fasten your seat belt, the armor of truth, and enjoy the ride.

It's important that you pay attention to what you're consuming. If you want to build your faith, you can't watch the news filled with stories of tragedy all day, or listen to your coworkers talk about how much they hate their lives. You must guard your heart.

"So, faith comes from hearing, and hearing through the word of Christ" (Romans 10:17 ESV).

We grow our faith by hearing, seeing, and breathing in the Word of God. Nothing else can give us confidence like the Word of God can. So, I ask you, what are you listening to? Are you listening to the Word of God or another source? I can guarantee you that if I were mediating on truth during that plane ride, I wouldn't have dreaded the worst because I would have kept God's truth at the forefront of my mind. If you are to live by faith, then you need to have faith; in order to have faith, you need to hear the Word of God.

It didn't work out "last time": Oftentimes, what has happened to us in our past can make us feel like nothing will ever work out for us. Maybe you didn't get into that school, or you prayed for a job that didn't hire you. Trust me, I understand those moments. But even if we can't see it, God chooses to work all those things out for our good. God knows when it's our time for certain doors to open, and He knows what's best for us. This reminds me of when the Lord brought me out of the financial turmoil that I was drowning in. He took me out of that hardship and brought me into a new season where He wanted me to believe Him for more. Because I saw so much turmoil in that year, it was hard to dust myself off again and have faith. I'm glad I believed God anyways because it opened up so many doors. The Lord is always taking us from one step of faith to another step of faith and our seasons are always changing. He's always making things new, so we can trust Him. We cannot allow what happened in our past hinder us from believing for what God shows us about our future. Our past does not dictate what our future will look like. We can have faith even if it didn't work out last time because of the Great God we serve.

Forgetting His Faithfulness: You have the power of choice. You can either choose to forget your past victories in Christ or engrave them in your mind. With the fast-track world that we live in, it can be easy to forget valuable truths. As Kingdom Daughters, we must remember our history with our Faithful God. Remember that school you were praying to get into? Remember that child you were believing God for? Remember the day you wanted to commit suicide? Remember His faithfulness. Allow yourself to revisit those moments where God saved you, restored you, and redeemed you. Let go of what you don't have and begin to praise Him for what you do have! Gratitude is a decision that you must make—in and out of season.

When is the last time that you sat and thanked God for what He's done? I dare you to do this with a sincere heart. A posture of gratitude will allow you to walk from faith to faith and to experience a life full of joy, love, and freedom.

I could go on about the many reasons why you may not trust the Lord, but the truth is that only you know what that reason is. Even if you're unsure, you can ask your gracious Heavenly Father; He will share. He knows you. Allow Him to lead you to a life of freedom and truth. I want you to know that you can't live a life of faith effectively unless you deal with the root issue of why you lack faith. Be brave enough to confront it. When you do, you will begin to experience a newfound freedom in Christ and live with confidence.

"My thoughts are nothing like your thoughts," says the Lord. "And my ways are far beyond anything you could imagine. For just as the heavens are higher than the earth, so are my ways higher than your ways, and my thoughts higher than your thoughts" (Isaiah 55:8-9 NLT).

Fight for Your Faith

Now that we've discovered some of the roots of our distrust, it's time to learn how to combat the doubt and fear. In order for us to fight against doubt, assumption, and lies of the enemy, we must properly arm and equip ourselves. Do you know that our faith is our actual armor and protection from the lies of the enemy (Ephesians 6:16)? Once we realize that our faith is our shield, there is nothing that the enemy can do to stop us.

Faith is like being on an airplane. You don't know what's coming up next, but there is someone who does—the pilot. He knows the destination, the arrival time, and he knows how to weather the storm. All the pilot really wants is for the passengers to sit back, relax, and enjoy the ride.

It's the same way with God. He knows when to take you in the mountains and lead you through the valleys. He knows how to prepare you for where you are going and how to land you safely into the promises He has for you. But just like you should trust your pilot, you must trust God, also. You must remember that God is perfect, meaning He makes no mistakes. Ever.

Maybe you need to re-learn this truth: God can be trusted. Maybe you're walking through some hard moments right now, and the truth seems hard to cling to. But you are never alone. If you want big faith, you must begin with where you are in your faith journey. Face the reality of where your faith is right now and ask the Lord for help. He's a gracious God. It is an act of humility to admit that you need more faith, you're weak, and you need to draw from His strength. Also, remember that faith is not trusting in what you can see. You're never going to find the faith that you need by looking at what you can see; you will find the faith that you need by keeping your eyes fixed on Jesus.

"Now our knowledge is partial and incomplete, and even the gift of prophecy reveals only part of the whole picture!"
(1 Corinthians 13:9 NLT)

God would never reveal all of His plans to you. Why? Because you were never created to know everything He knows. We were created to be children living under a perfect Heavenly Father; we were never created to be apart from Him. Therefore, you're designed to be attached and submitted to God, wholly and fully. But in order for you to fully trust His fatherhood and leadership, you must learn His nature. From that place, you will grow in faith and learn to trust His goodness. Your confidence in God—His goodness, His sovereignty, His leadership, His plan, and His fatherhood—is the foundation for everything you believe as a Christian.

Thank God, He has given us this beautiful gift of faith! He is able to cultivate your faith through different seasons and circumstances. God will teach you how to have faith.

"Now faith is the substance of things hoped for, the evidence of things not seen" (Hebrews 11:1 NKJV).

It is not by anything that you see that gives you faith. You shouldn't trust in what is seen, but rather what is unseen. You can be surrounded by your situation, but your faith will enable you to believe that God will see you through. Your faith is like an anchor that drops down deep into the waters of uncertainty, and when the wind and waves come, you are unmovable. But your faith is also like muscle; if you're not exercising it, it will not grow. You have to continue to work out your faith muscles by passing the tests that come your way—even the little ones.

"Oh yeah, I tried that faith thing, and it didn't work," you might say.

No. With anything, you have to exert effort to make it work. Sometimes, you need to go the extra mile. You have to stare fear straight in the face and tell it to move! Maybe you need to pull out those notecards and memorize scripture. Try waking up an hour earlier in the morning to pray. Do you want to be more confident and bold in your faith? That takes persistent effort and self-discipline. That is what I did. I had to get out of the shallow end of my faith and press deeper. I declared truth over my life!

I want you to say this declaration with me:

God, I will not be moved by what I can see. Your faithfulness is my confidence! I know You are My Helper in my time of need, and I will not be distracted by what the world tells me. God, thank You that you've given me Your eyes to see my life. I trust You to see me through this. I know that You will never forsake me. Thank You that You've given me the power and strength to use my shield of faith to fight. I will trust in Your Word and hold tightly to Your promises. In Jesus' name I pray, Amen.

These are the types of truths you must declare over yourself, your family, and your friends. You have permission to use the faith that God has given you, and you don't have to wait to start having faith. You can start right now. Even if you've been full of doubt, there's room for you, too. Be that brave, courageous woman you've always wanted to be. You do not have to spin out of control when the doubt, worry, or fear tries to make its way in. You can stand as a confident daughter, knowing that your Father will always have your back. There *are* some practical things we can do to build our faith and I thought it be cool to share a few of them with you. Here are three ways you can build your faith:

Consistently getting in the presence of God: You should never pull away from God's presence when you're lacking faith. You should enter into His presence more. Much like I mentioned earlier, our faith grows the more we use it. It is the same way with getting into the presence of God; the more we press in, the more confident we are in our faith. Nothing can grow if it's not being watered. Your faith grows and is able to be nourished and refreshed when you draw from the never-ending Well (Jesus). But you must keep drawing from that Well every single day. Consistency will build your confidence.

Ask and You Shall Receive: In James 1:5, God tells us that if we lack wisdom, we can go to Him and He will give it to us. There's nothing that God wants to hide from us—especially stronger faith. The times when I was at my lowest, I had to humble myself and ask the Lord, "God please help my unbelief." I want you to know that there's nothing wrong with that. The Lord knows your heart and He knows where you are, so honesty is exactly what He desires from you. You might think it's almost like "cheating" to ask God for faith to believe, but I challenge you to ask Him. He's faithful to respond.

Work your Faith: The only way you will know what you're made of is if you begin to use it. I believe that's why God places us in certain situations. It's as if He's saying, "come on daughter, you can do this, show Me what you've learned." He's that dad that stands at the finish line waiting for you, cheering you on. He doesn't want you to lose; He wants you to win. He'll send little reminders along the way so you don't grow weary. So, sister work your faith. Your Father wants you to be great and go higher—I dare you to step out.

"So, do not be afraid, Jacob, my servant; do not be dismayed, Israel," says the Lord (Jeremiah 30:10 NLT).

CHAPTER SEVEN:

The Roadblock of Offense

What if you're on this faith walk and nothing is working out? It seems like every door you want to open is being shut. Then what? Do you turn away? Do you give up? Or do you keep saying yes to God? We've all heard about offense in our hearts towards people, but what if you find yourself with offense in your heart towards God? Offense tries to seep into the hearts of Christians, especially in the midst of a hard season. We begin to question His goodness, character, and nature. It can bring about apathy and complacency. For starters, let's define offense.

Offense is defined as: an *annoyance or resentment brought about by a perceived insult to or disregard for oneself or one's standards or principles.*

"But Jasmine," you ask, "how can that be? How can we as Christians have offense in our hearts towards God?" So often, offense can come into our hearts when we begin to question who God is, and what He is doing in our lives. There's a difference between asking questions and questioning someone. Asking questions is simply requesting information. Questioning is when you begin to challenge someone's character.

Mary, the mother of Jesus asked questions simply for more information. She asked, *"But how can this be? I'm a virgin"* (Luke 1:34 NLT). Mary wasn't doubting God's nature or the promise, she was just requesting more information about *how* a baby would be conceived from her *virgin* womb. Questioning looks something like this: *"How can I be sure this will happen? I'm an old man now, and my wife is also well along in years"* (Luke 1:18 NLT). This was a question that Zechariah asked the Lord after He had just promised Zechariah a son, who would be John the Baptist. Zechariah questioned God from a place of doubt, wanting the Lord to reassure him of the blessing. This was a *question of doubt* because in verse twenty, the angel says, *"since you **didn't believe** what I said, you will be silent and unable to speak until the child is born. For my words will certainly be fulfilled at the proper time"* (Luke 1:20 NLT). We must be careful not to *question* God or His nature.

There was a time when marriage and having a family consumed my mind. So much so that I began to want it more than anything else—even more than an intimate relationship with the Lord. Being married became a *huge* distraction in my heart, and it slowly became all I thought about. For me, I didn't want to serve the One I proclaimed to trust because I felt like He was withholding from me—this is where offense entered in. If I could put words to my offense it would be, *"God, You're not moving fast enough and I don't think Your timing is fair!"* My fire for God slowly dwindled away as I pushed His voice that whispered, *"Trust Me"* out with my own doubt and insecurities. Sometimes unbelief is the doorway to offense and it slowly creeps in when we're the most vulnerable.

In this place in my life, I didn't really have much—barely affording groceries, gas, or basic necessities. I had just moved to Atlanta by faith, I immediately ran into financial difficulties, and life was just getting hard. During this time, I was pulling more away from God than I was reading my Word, spending time in prayer, and worshipping. When I avoided the pain in my heart, offense towards God began to take place. Instead of going to God in prayer about my frustrations, I backed away. I felt like He no longer saw me or cared about me. This idea only came because I placed my eyes on my circumstances *more* than on the God who could change them. Now, I see that this is exactly what the enemy wanted for my life—space between God and I. The enemy's plan for us is to distance us from God, make up lies, and turn us away from God. My friend, this is the danger of not drenching yourself with the Word and prayer: you lose sight of who God really is.

Maybe that's you. Maybe you find yourself questioning God's goodness in your life. Maybe you've pulled back from Him. Maybe you're even in ministry, but you've just lost your faith. Maybe something happened in your life and now you hold an offense in your heart towards God.

I want you to know that there's grace even for being in this place. God *wants* to help walk you out of this place and to be able to see Him through the correct lens. Not only that, but I believe He wants to show you that He so deeply cares about every situation you go through. He's not mad at your questions and doubts. He doesn't want you to remain in a place of frustration and hopelessness. He wants to help you believe again. He wants you to trust Him again. For me, it took spending intentional time in the Word and being around community to really break down the wall of offense I had put up against God.

GOD IS *GOOD!* I'll declare that for the rest of my life, no matter what I face. I want you to know that for yourself. Together, I want to dive into some ways we can avoid offense in our hearts towards God and how to combat offense if you find yourself in this place.

Is God withholding from me? Maybe your story is different from mine. Maybe your offense developed from an absent father, maybe from an empty ring finger, maybe from a closed door on a school you wanted to attend—but I want to challenge you with this: *We are oftentimes offended by what we do not understand.* If you look at Genesis chapter three, you see from the beginning that the enemy wanted to breed offense in our hearts towards God by illuminating what we didn't understand. God wasn't withholding any *good* thing from us even from the Garden of Eden. He was protecting us from danger. We have to remember that God created us, so He knows what's good for us and what is not. Our job is to trust that He knows exactly what He's doing.

I know this is easier said than done, but unbelief, distrust, and offense draw us away from the Father. We can know that God would never withhold any good thing from us because He didn't withhold salvation from us. This is how we can *know* He is good! He came to save us. If He didn't love us or have good plans for us, He wouldn't have sent His son to the Cross so we could live in freedom. He will always give us what we need, and He will never withhold any good thing from us (Philippians 4:19). In fact, His Word says:

> *"For the Lord God is our sun and our shield.*
> *He gives us grace and glory.*

The Lord will withhold no good thing
from those who do what is right" (Psalm 84:11 NLT).

Serving God before man: Serving man before God is one of the biggest ways we can lose our wonder in the Lord. It is the driving force behind believers who typically leave the church, stop reading the Word, or pull away from the faith altogether.

Our priority must always be God first, people second. I've seen it happen: someone who may be serving in church gets offended by another believer. From there, they may pull back from the mission, attend another church or sadly even leave the faith altogether. So, why is it so important to serve God before people? Because serving people *first* causes you to become a people-pleaser. And people pleasing leads to disappointment. One thing we must know about people is that they are fickle; they're always changing. The Bible says that they are as frail as breath (Isaiah 2:22 NLT). Not only that, but people are also draining. If we place our hope in the people we are serving, we will always be disappointed.

Disappointment kills our drive for the things of God. I ask you to examine your heart. Do you carry unforgiveness, resentment, or even offense in your heart towards anyone in your life? I want you to know that it doesn't matter what position you're in—pastor, worship leader, volunteer—we all have to address these things. If we place our hope in the people we are serving, we will always be disappointed. God wants our service to be for Him alone. This is why the Bible teaches us that we are to work unto Him in every area of our lives (Colossians 3:23). When we gaze upon who He is, we can be full enough to pour out to those around us in an effective way. He is our source and strength and servanthood begins with Him. If we prioritize God, our labor will never be in vain.

Trust God's timing: Trusting God's timing is a vital part of our relationship with the Lord. If not careful, distrusting God's timing will lead to jealously, frustration, bitterness and offense towards God.

Meet Kayla. She works for a marketing company and loves what she does. She attends church on a regular basis and even serves as one of the leaders in her church. Kayla's friend Sarah is about to get married. Just like Kayla, Sarah loves the Lord and attends church on a regular basis. But because God has introduced Sarah's husband to her, Kayla is filled with bitterness and jealously. She struggles to believe that God's timing is accurate and God will fulfill the desire in her heart. Kayla is so frustrated that she believes she should have gotten married *before* Sarah. Because Kayla hasn't addressed the issues in her heart, she now has pursued a relationship with a man that she knows isn't right for her because she feels neglected by God.

This is just one example, but do you see how *one little issue* can run you on a course of offense if not quickly confronted? We as daughters must *humble* ourselves and trust that God chooses when we receive certain things. We must stay in position as daughters and let God be God. God has made everything appropriate for your life.

*"He has made everything **appropriate** in its time. He has also set eternity in their heart, yet so that man will not find out the work which God has done from the beginning even to the end"* (Ecclesiastes 3:11 NASB).

Trusting God's Sovereignty: What do you think of when you hear the words, "God is sovereign?" Maybe you think of words like, power, ruler, authority, or control. All of these things illustrate who God is. He is all-powerful, He has all authority, and He is in-control. I believe that we lose sight of this truth when we face different circumstances. Maybe you recently lost a loved one, maybe your ex broke your heart, or maybe you're facing bankruptcy and don't know what to do. I can't imagine the pain you're facing, but I want you to know that God is with you. Even the losses we experience that seem unfair or don't make sense to us are under God's control. That may not change how you feel and that's understandable, but I want you to know that you can find rest and comfort in the sovereignty and justice of God. He never misses anything and He will always repay.

"Dear friends, never take revenge. Leave that to the righteous anger of God. For the Scriptures say, 'I will take revenge; I will pay them back,' says the Lord."
(Romans 12:19 NLT).

Job lost everything: his wife, his children, his money, his job—everything. But even still, he never once turned away. Job *chose* to remain faithful *even while* battling doubt. Job creates a model that we could learn from. No matter what we face, we can lean on these truths and His Word when the temptation of *"is this really worth it?"* tries to invade our minds. We will choose to believe God is just. We will choose to believe God is faithful. We will choose to believe that God is merciful. And we will believe all these things by faith.

I encourage you to learn more about who God is in His Word. This will eliminate the false ideas of who He is that we conjure up when faced with hardship, tests, or trials. Meditate on this scripture:

> *"To whom will you compare me? Who is my equal?" asks the Holy One. Look up into the heavens. Who created all the stars? He brings them out like an army, one after another, calling each by its name. Because of his great power and incomparable strength, not a single one is missing. O Jacob, how can you say the Lord does not see your troubles? O Israel, how can you say God ignores your rights? Have you never heard? Have you never understood? The Lord is the everlasting God, the Creator of all the earth. He never grows weak or weary. No one can measure the depths of his understanding. He gives power to the weak and strength to the powerless. Even youths will become weak and tired, and young men will fall in exhaustion. But those who trust in the Lord will find new strength. They will soar high on wings like eagles. They will run and not grow weary. They will walk and not faint* (Isaiah 40:25-31 NLT).

CHAPTER EIGHT

The Roadblock of Lust

One of the greatest adversaries against this generation of women is lust. Lust is no respecter of persons; it will live anywhere it is entertained. God has created us for His idea of marriage, sex, and a family—that is the order. If lust can corrupt the perfect union between God, man, and woman, it will (Genesis 2:18). If a woman can give into sexual temptation, she devalues her God-crafted body, bringing potential harm to it. This could lead to *sexually transmitted diseases, babies out of wedlock,* and *soul ties.* These are just a *few* of the things that come from lust. Lust baits you with pleasure and indulgence, but it traps you with shame and defeat. It does not tell you about the consequences beforehand because it wants pleasure and it wants it now.

If you find yourself with any of these consequences, I want you to know that God is the God of *restoration.* He's faithful and just to forgive and restore you when you confess your sins to Him. His grace covers you even when you have the STD, the baby out of wedlock, and so on. When you decide to live for Him, but you carry scars from the past, you must understand that He doesn't remove

His love from you. He still loves you. There's nothing that God can't heal, no heart that He can't mend, and no soul tie He can't destroy. Believe these truths as we dive a little deeper in this chapter.

Lust does not care how old you are, how much money you make, or how long you've been saved; it will patiently dangle the bait before you in hopes to lead you further and further away from God. Giving in to sexual temptation will open doors that will pull you out of the safety and protection of the Father's will. Pleasure and sex are not *bad things*. They're *good thing*s when they're done God's way. God's way protects from pain, confusion, and/or heartbreak. God wants His children to be safe, and in order to do that, He sets up *boundaries* inside His Word for us to live by. These boundaries are not to be mistaken for *restrictions*. God doesn't keep good things from us, but He does have us wait for *His* timing to fulfill certain desires (Psalm 84:11). These boundaries allow us to enjoy pleasures that God has given us peacefully in each season of our lives. I like to think of these boundaries as a roadmap to know which path to take and which path to avoid. God perfectly orchestrates a map for you and allows you to walk along the best path for your life (Psalm 32:8). We can rest in the fact that God will always lead us to good. I don't know about you, but I long to be under the protection of God in every area of my life. I've journeyed out of His protection before, and it never led to anything good.

If this is your struggle and you are in the midst of lust right now, I want you to know that you are not alone. Maybe you've tried to break away from pornography for years and nothing has changed. Maybe you've tried to stop fornication and you keep going in circles. If that is you, I want you to know there is grace for you and God desires for you to be free. God wants to show you a way out. Sister, there is a way out, even if you don't see it right now. There is nothing impossible for God, I want you to know that. The good news is that we can overcome *any* temptation we may face, even sexual ones. Notice I said we can overcome the *temptation*—that does not mean we will not have to *face* them on a daily basis. You may never stop being tempted, but you can learn to overcome. Within this chapter, I hope to teach you Biblical ways to overcome the roadblock of lust.

1) *Surround yourself with community* – If you find yourself walking alone through an addiction of any sort, I want to encourage you to get around people you can be honest with. Maybe confide in your pastor, your friend, your small group, etc. You need at least one person keeping you accountable. They are able to equip you with the armor that you need to fight back and help strengthen you in areas you are weak in. Not only that, but they can cover you in prayer on a consistent basis. Because this battle is a spiritual one, you are going to want people to fight this battle with you (Ephesians 6:12).

When I opened up to a friend about my addiction, I remember feeling free just by sharing what I had hidden for so many years. I no longer felt like I had to walk alone anymore. In fact, it gave me the confidence to want to leave it behind altogether. Do you have a community of believers around you? If you don't, you should. It's okay to be a little nervous about sharing, but don't let that hold you back from seeking help. There is strength in numbers and we were created for relationships. I don't care what your title is, if you are a Christian blogger, if you are in ministry, if you are a leader in your church—seek help! We have all fallen short, so know that God's grace is there to catch you (Romans 3:23). Once you open up, you will find that freedom was easier than you had ever imagined—all because of community.

"So, whether you eat or drink, or whatever you do, do it all for the glory of God" (1 Corinthians 10:31 NLT).

2) *Our breakthrough is to ultimately bring God glory* — When I first began trying to break free from my addiction, I tried to break free for all the wrong reasons. I was more concerned about how I would be viewed if someone knew about it than I was pleasing God. I was more worried about getting caught in the act by *man*, than realizing that I was hurting God while looking at those

videos. Whether it be fornication, masturbation, adultery, homosexuality, porn, or anything else, you might be wondering how you can break free. But you have to remember that when you do anything, even breaking from a stronghold, it is solely for the glory of God. He is the one we are aiming to please—not ourselves, not other people. It isn't about being able to count the number of days it's been since "we did it," it's about keeping our gaze on the One we want to please the most. This perspective allows us to remember our **why** throughout the process; it teaches us to lean and depend only on Him.

3) *We can overcome **with** Jesus*—I had a girlfriend tell me once that she keeps going back to the same guy and falling into sexual sin with him. She didn't understand why it was so hard to break free. It wasn't long before she was once again making promises to never go back to him. I could tell she was trying to fight in her flesh (trying to avoid spending time with him, promising *herself* she'd never go back to him,

etc.) But the issue wasn't that she couldn't break free, it was that she hadn't let Jesus **fully** in on the process of emancipation. During this time, she wasn't spending much time with God and she was still teetering with the thought of going back to him. While we will never be perfect, it is very important that we surrender completely to God in the process of breaking free. We must do things His way, not our way.

"And they overcame him by the blood of the Lamb, and by the word of their testimony; and they loved not their lives unto death" (Revelation 12:11 NKJV).

It doesn't matter what your stronghold is, you can't overcome any other way but *with* Jesus. The first part of this verse says that *by the blood of the lamb.* The Lamb is Jesus Christ our Savior. He not only promises to save us, but He also promised to continue to save us from our sinful nature as we live on this Earth. He promises to save us from our sinful nature by walking with us each and every second of the day to help lead us into a life of righteousness. The Bible teaches us that God's Spirit, or the Holy Spirit, is our helper (John 14:26). When you feel lost, the Holy Spirit is there to help guide along the right path. It's important when breaking free that you don't ignore the Holy Spirit's lead.

*"But the Holy Spirit produces this kind of fruit in our lives: love, joy, peace, patience, kindness, goodness, faithfulness, gentleness and **self-control**"*
(Galatians 5:22-23 NLT).

If you want to end the raging war of sexual sin in your life, you are going to have to follow the Holy Spirit. And in order to follow His lead, you must spend time with Him. We are to be led by the Holy Spirit in all things, but *especially* when fighting off temptation. So, what is your struggle? Are you inviting God fully into the process, or are you fighting in your flesh? Have you surrendered all to Him? Invite Jesus into your emancipation process; be open and vulnerable about your weaknesses and He will be faithful to help you.

4) Digging up the roots—Our sin struggles always stem from a root issue. Besides sin being in our nature because of the fall of Adam and Eve, some of us have faced real traumatic experiences growing up that have shaped our idea of sex. I know for me, it was the girls in my school that exposed me to porn at a young age that made me view sex completely differently than I do now. As I was in the process of growing closer to God, He had to uproot some things in my heart and remove some labels I had placed on myself. For example, I used to never see myself as being a godly wife because I was so used to temporary relationships. Those relationships only revolved around **one thing.** I began to place this *"damaged goods"* label on myself and this led to me settling for less than God's best—even after I gave my life to Christ.

My past experiences shaped my perception of my identity in Christ and my value in Him, which led me down paths of chaos. Thankfully, God is a restorer and He began to show me that **I am** worthy because of the cross. He reminded me that I was still called to receive His best in every area of my life. This same truth applies to you!

It breaks my heart to see so many women completely devalue themselves with sex—whether it's homosexuality, porn, masturbation, fornication, or more, because they do not fully understand the underlying cause for their actions. If this is you, I ask that you go before the Father in prayer and ask Him *why* you keep returning to your sin. Let Him heal you in that place. Sometimes, God has to reach back and heal the younger version of yourself that was stripped of your innocence at a young age in order for you to finally see what the root issue is. It takes courage to get to this place, but in the end, it is worth it. He will be faithful to meet with you and help you overcome, no matter what your past looked like.

5) *Know your triggers*—In this last section, I want to leave you with some practical tips to *fight back*. The truth is, since you are a daughter of the King, you are going to get tested over and over

again because you are a target to the enemy. The enemy would love nothing more than to place that guy or those videos in your pathway to cause you to stumble, but you will overcome in Jesus' name.

Ask yourself this: what do you realize about yourself right before you fall into sexual sin? What emotions do you experience? Are you sad? Angry? Where are you usually at? For me, I was always sad, upset, or lonely.

When you begin to feel those emotions rising up, this should be your indicator that it is time to pray and spend time with the Lord. He will help you to fight back and help you unpack your emotions. Sexual sins always want to lead us into temporary fixes—don't fall for it. The Lord promises to give us full satisfaction when we're in His presence. A lot of times, we can overcome the battle simply by using wisdom. If you know you struggle with it when you're by yourself, then maybe you should start surrounding yourself more with other believers. Or maybe you begin to crave it after that reality

TV show where all they do is kiss—turn it OFF! Or maybe it's the late-night conversations on the phone with that guy—try not to be on the phone late. The Lord gives us wisdom to use in case-by-case scenarios, and when we don't know what to do, He is faithful to show us.

Know that you are a daughter of God and He doesn't want you to live in bondage, but in freedom. I spent a decade of my life living as a slave to sexual sin, and while I am thankful God redeems and restores time, I wish I hadn't traveled down that path. Don't believe the lie that you will always be like this; you are free! I am a living testament of this. Know that I am standing in agreement with you. Don't grow weary in the fight. God is with you and He's on your side. This will no longer be the roadblock you have to face. You are free. In Jesus' name.

"So, if the Son sets you free, you will be free indeed"
(John 8:36 NIV).

CHAPTER NINE:

The Roadblock of Shame

Usually when we've lived in a place of sinful pursuit, it makes us feel embarrassed and ashamed. I've met some of the most powerful people in the Kingdom of God who still struggle with shame even though they no longer pursue a sinful lifestyle. This truly breaks my heart because we fail to understand the *free* gift that has been given to us because of Jesus. When a gift is given by a father, it is meant to be accepted and enjoyed right away. It is not to be placed on the shelf for the recipient to question whether they can truly accept it. I mean, who wouldn't enjoy a gift from a *good father*—especially if that father knows exactly what his child needs and desires? But how many of us place grace on the shelf to stare at our sins, not embracing the gift God has given us? How many of us truly understand grace?

When I think of the word *grace*, I think of God's unending, unconditional love for you and I. This grace doesn't end when we find ourselves at rock-bottom and it doesn't begin when we feel like we have it all together. It is a constant pouring out of a love that we may never be able to comprehend in this life. Even when we can't make sense of it,

God only asks us to receive it. No matter what our pasts looks like, no matter where we've been, He just asks us to receive it.

To be honest, as believers, we are very quick to declare forgiveness and grace over someone else's life, yet we can't receive it for our own lives. Sometimes, not fully accepting that we are saved, redeemed, and set free by grace and grace alone can hinder us from going deeper with the Lord. We end up stumbling upon shame and get defeated because we look back on our regrets that have already been washed by the blood. Jesus didn't die on the cross and rise from the grave to save some of us; He came to redeem and restore *all of us*. Yet, we try to work so hard for a gift that was never ours to earn in the first place. Grace is not grace if you have to work for it. Though God's grace is sometimes unbelievable, we can receive it and enjoy it.

"God saved you by his grace when you believed. And you can't take credit for this; it is a gift from God"
(Ephesians 2:8 NLT).

One day, I was over a friend's house, and a huge weight of insecurity fell upon me as I sat and watched other women *my age* playing with their babies while their husbands fellowshipped. It was a beautiful picture of how I wanted my life to be, but it quickly turned into jealously, frustration, and insecurity. I began to ask myself, "why am I not married yet?" All these thoughts began to rush in, and right before I went off the deep end, I heard the Lord gently set me free with this truth. He said, "you know none of these women deserved it, right?"

Talk about a tear-jerking statement! I knew immediately what He meant. He was saying that none of those women who were playing joyfully with their children did anything to deserve a husband and family. God did **not** say, "hey, only you guys can have children, but if you have a horrible past, you cannot receive it."

He also didn't say, "hey, if you have had a horrible past, then just be single for decades, because it's going to take forever for you to heal. I need to clean you up first."

Isn't that the lie we oftentimes believe? That somehow God is withholding from us because of our pasts? And that, if you have a family, a husband, a great career, God is more pleased with you than everyone else. We must be **very careful** to not think that forgiveness equates to blessings. You are blessed because you are forgiven. In God's timing and through His grace, God allows you to enjoy those other blessings. But please don't think that you aren't in the will of God because you don't have what other women have. God will give you the desires of your heart as you delight in Him and in His *perfect* timing (Psalm 37:4). Grace is not something that can be earned and if you had to be perfect in order to receive those things, nobody would have them. God doesn't choose those who are deserving; He chooses the ones who are the least deserving. Let's look at this verse:

"Though I am the least deserving of all God's people, he graciously gave me the privilege of telling the Gentiles about the endless treasures available to them in Christ"
(Ephesians 3:8 NLT).

Let's unpack this verse. First off, Paul was a giant for the Kingdom of God, but prior to serving the Lord, He was a murderer. He killed Christians, yet God still picked Him to carry His name. Look at this first part of the verse, it says, "though I am the least deserving..." then, if you skip a few words down it says, "he graciously gave..." So, we see two things: Paul was the least deserving and that God still gave to him. Paul is the perfect image of God's grace for us. God completely redeemed and restored his life and all Paul did was say yes! Not only that, but God was ready to use Paul once he surrendered.

For some of you, you may read his story and think, "I get it. I believe God worked in Paul's life, but what about me? What about my past?" You may find it hard to believe God's grace for you, especially after living the lifestyle you lived. Or maybe there's been a more recent mistake that you made that you wish you hadn't. God's mercy knows no end. This means that the grace of God can meet us in the middle of our greatest mistakes. I want you right now to think about the worst mistake that you've ever made. Got it? Imagine God taking that mistake and throwing it into the sea of forgetfulness. This sea represents the mercy and grace of God. Not one of our sins are ever held over our heads *when* we confess them. Many of you have been seeking that confirmation that God has forgiven you and this is it. Your sins *have been forgiven* and He remembers them no more (Hebrews 8:12).

"You will again have compassion on us; you will tread our sins underfoot and hurl all our iniquities into the depths of the sea" (Micah 7:19 NIV).

God isn't holding anything over your head. He wants to lift your head so that you know that you are forgiven, loved, and redeemed. For many of us, this is the nasty lie we believe— "God is holding my sins against me." I challenge you to ask yourself *why* you think He is holding something against you. This lie goes directly against the nature of who God is. He is faithful, He is kind, and He is just. Perhaps you've been hurt by people who haven't easily forgiven you and that's why you don't think God has forgiven you. Sometimes, we place labels on God because of the way we view people. But God is not a person. He is a perfect God and a perfect Father. Even if you made a thousand mistakes, it still wouldn't be enough to take His love away from you.

It's really not about how much you've done in your past, it's about how much He did on the cross.

As I watched those women play with their babies, I began to remember these women's stories and how God brought them out of their lifestyles and made *all things* new. There were women there that have lived lifestyles of alcoholism, partying, sex outside of marriage, and addictions. God makes all things new for all of us, not just some of us. He has good plans for *you*.

I remember one day just looking back on how far God has truly brought me. I remember feeling so full of shame and hopelessness, but then the Lord stepped in and changed everything. He took this girl who used to be afraid to even open her mouth, and put her on a stage to lead worship. He took this girl who used to live under the shade of shame and gave her purpose to heal with words. He gave this girl a brand-new meaning for life, when there once were days she didn't want to live. Don't discount yourself because of your past. There is a plan that God has for you and it is beyond your wildest dreams. I dare you to ask God what new things He wants to do in you. Don't be afraid, sister. He doesn't want to hide His amazing plans from you. He wants to show you them so that you will walk in them. Sometimes, it's a process to see the plans that God has for you. It slowly unravels as we submit ourselves to His will and His timing. Be patient as the Lord works out His good plans for you. He *will* work out His plans for you (Psalm 138:8).

Don't ever allow the enemy to deceive you. He wants you to think you're not forgiven so that you don't walk into the freedom that God has available for you. The enemy distracts you from God's bright future by making you dwell on the past. But your past no longer defines you. God has branded you with *His* name.

March out in *victory*, daughters! Sing your songs of praise to the King! He has *saved* you, *redeemed* you, and *called you* by name. You *will* fulfill all that God has for you. You will be *bold* and *courageous* and you will begin using your past as your weapon. Your story is a *weapon* against the enemy's camp that will impact *nations*. Satan is *afraid* of you. Be that version of yourself that you've always wanted to be, not the one that wants to *run and hide*. You have been called for such a time as this. The world is looking for *your story*, *your calling*, and *your voice*. Today, shame meets face-to-face with grace. Today you will come back to the Father and know without a shadow of a doubt that you belong, and that He loves you! If you've been dealing with fear and shame, I declare over you that today you are free in Jesus' name!

> *Father, I pray over my sisters right now. I ask that Your hand of victory would lift them out of the pit of shame and defeat. I thank You that you have not*

given them a spirit of FEAR but of power, love, and a sound mind. I speak to the girl who has been afraid to walk out her calling because of her past. I thank You Father that she is no longer on the sidelines, but that she rises to be who You've called her to be. I prophesy, Father, that each individual that reads this book will be set free; that You would continue to help them recognize their freedom. Holy Spirit dwell in their homes, schools, cars—cover them and help them to use YOUR WORDS to fight back against the enemy's lies and deceit. I declare the lie of shame ends today. Satan, you have no authority and you have no place in these girls' lives. I bind you up in the name of Jesus. They wear the banner of GRACE and NOT shame because of the blood of Jesus Christ. I declare freedom over them right now and I thank You Jesus in advance for it. In Jesus' name, Amen.

CHAPTER TEN:

The Road to Redemption

"So now there is no condemnation for those who belong to Christ Jesus" (Romans 8:1 NLT).

I knew a man in his forties who struggled in his faith. All his life he knew of God, having been raised in church, but somewhere in the midst of life, he turned away from pursuing God. This led him into relationships he shouldn't have entered into, and left him feeling purposeless. It wasn't long before he started to feel empty. One day he opened up to me about his desire to learn more about God. I shared my story, he shared his, and by the grace of God, seeds were planted.

A few weeks passed and he told me that he had rededicated his life to Christ. Weeks after that, he went to church for the first time in a while. All of this brought him to one defining moment in his faith. He came to me some days later with such a joy on his face and said, "It's so crazy, I thought this whole time God was mad at me and I learned that *He's not!*"

I thought to myself, *no wonder this man was hesitant about God! He assumed that God was somehow mad at him for the way he lived most of his life.* His paradigm blew me away. I couldn't help but think about other wayward Christians. What were their questions? Did they think God was mad at them, too? Did they assume the road to redemption would be too messy? Were they too condemned to even try?

The most common misconception about our faith in Jesus Christ is that somehow you no longer are welcome into a relationship with God because you've had a messy past. But this is the very reason why Jesus went to the cross—to reconcile our relationship with God. It is in His *very nature* to redeem and restore. Suppose you've had an addiction; He wants to restore you. Suppose you've spent years behind bars; He has good plans for you. He has a beautiful plan for *everyone,* there's no one that is excluded from His redemption plan, not even you. We can find God's heart for redemption in Luke 15, where we learn about the prodigal son's life. Let's read about God's heart for redemption.

A man had two sons, and he was divvying up his estate between the two of them. The younger son wanted his share immediately; he decided he didn't want to wait. So, the dad gave him his portion. A few days after this, the younger son packed all his belongings and moved to a distant land. In this distant land, he wasted all his money in wild living. Around this time, a great famine covered the land he was in. He began to **starve.** He tried to make things work out, so he persuaded a local farmer to hire him. But even still, he didn't have enough. The same food he gave the pigs he desired to eat as well (Luke 15:16).

We eventually see that the son comes to his senses and realizes that he wants to be home. So, the son journeyed home. There, he was showered with grace:

> *"So, he returned home to his father. And while he was still a long way off, his father saw him coming. Filled with love and compassion, **he ran to his son**, embraced him and kissed him. His son said to him, 'Father, I have sinned against both heaven and you, and I am no longer worthy of being called your son.' But the father said to the servants, 'Quick! Bring the finest robe in the house and put it on him. Get a ring for his finger and sandals for his feet. And*

kill the calf we have been fattening. **We must celebrate** *with a feast, for this son of mine was dead and has now returned to life. He was lost, but now he* **is found**.*' So, the party began"* (John 15:20-24 NLT).

The truth is, the son had a choice on whether he would live a life pleasing unto his father or live for the world. He made his choice, but even when he made the wrong choice, he was met with grace. Maybe you find yourself wondering, "how did I get to this place?" You find yourself in the thick mud of your mistakes and you want to come out. "Does God still love me? Will He still accept me if I come back?" You may not be brave enough to share these questions with others, but in your heart, you've asked them. Even when you are living outside of God's perfect will, you can still return. There is *nothing* that can separate you from the love of God.

"And I am convinced that nothing can ever separate us from God's love. Neither death nor life, neither angels nor demons, neither our fears for today nor our worries about tomorrow—

not even the powers of hell can separate us from God's love"

(Romans 8:38-39 NLT).

I've asked myself some of these similar questions and I want to share with you some of the truths of God's nature that brought me hope, joy, and assurance that God still loved me despite my deepest, darkest mistakes.

God is always ready to forgive—In verse 21, we see the son was very sorry about all of his mistakes. This was his confession of his sins. And in the very next verse, the father quickly responds with grace by grabbing him the finest robe, a ring on his finger and sandals for his feet. The father didn't push him away because he made some mistakes—he embraced him. This is a picture of grace. No matter what you have done, know that God is always ready to forgive you when you confess your sins to Him.

"But if we confess our sins to him, he is faithful and just to forgive us our sins and cleanse us from all wickedness"

(1 John 1:9 NLT).

God never holds anything over our heads—I love that the father was so ready to shower his son with gifts and even throw him a welcome-home party! Notice he didn't say, "son where have you been? Why did you leave?" or try to throw shame in his face. No. He welcomed him in and knew exactly what he needed. Be encouraged that God never holds anything over your head. He's always ready to finish the work He began in you, no matter what detours you may have taken. If this is you, know that God is ready to move forward and walk you into the new life He has for you. Be confident that He's not withholding from you. He loves you.

God will finish what He began in you— Oftentimes, we can feel like the road to redemption will be too long or too much work. While I can't promise it won't be long or challenging, I can assure you that God will complete what He's began in you. Everyone's story of coming back Home will be different, but God will finish what He started in *you*. The beautiful part about having a relationship with God is that He does all the cleaning for you. Our job is to just submit to the process He takes us on. I believe that the prodigal son's greatest fear was that he would have to start over. But as we can tell by the story, starting over was the best decision he could have ever made.

So, no matter where you may find yourself, know that the grace of God is available to you. He is waiting to meet you halfway as you run towards the place where you belong. He wants to embrace you again. He wants you to know Him again. He wants you to love Him again. Instead of thinking, "I'm a lost cause and there's no hope for me," think, "I am loved, I am redeemed, and God will restore my life."

"...Turn me again to you and restore me, for you alone are the Lord my God" (Jeremiah 31:18 NLT).

CHAPTER ELEVEN:

The Path

As I was writing this book, I looked back to my old journals, and I noticed how the pages were filled with wisdom, revelation, and knowledge. I was learning and growing so much. But as I began to pay closer attention to my *other* entries, I noticed that several pages were filled with, "God, where are you?" or "How am I going to pay this bill?" or even statements about not hearing God's voice at all. Unbelief, assumptions, and questions flooded the pages of my journals. In fact, here is a sample of one of those entries:

April 2014:

"I am sorry again. I want to move forward with You! I want to just trust You regardless of what's been going on. God, why can't I believe You have a plan for me? Help me to change my attitude. I don't always want to be depressed and down. I've laid my desires down at Your feet and I have no idea when You're going to open a door...."

During this time, I was walking through my senior year of college. This was one month away from graduation and I still hadn't found a job like the rest of my classmates. In fact, I had received over twenty or more rejection letters from companies by email. I truly felt defeated and overlooked by God. I wish I could tell myself then to just rest, trust, be still and know that He is God and He is GOOD. I didn't understand that the *path* that God was leading me on would be the very path to *help my unbelief.* Even with the closed doors, He was beginning to seal the gap in my faith. I was beginning to go from *head* knowledge to *knowing* in my heart He's good. I had always heard He was good, but *this path* He took me on would be the one to believe that truth for myself. Even though on the outside it looked like I was flourishing in my walk with the Lord, because I was blogging and sharing my faith on social media, but on the inside, I was filled with unbelief and brokenness. During this time, I felt like I had no other choice but to depend on God. I carried so much baggage from my past that God decided it was time to get real and unpack before Him.

The truth is, many of us give our hearts to Christ, but where most of us get stuck is surrendering to *the path* He has chosen for us. Maybe the path He has you on is teaching you how to wait on Him, or maybe He wants you to trust Him with your finances, or maybe like the Israelites, He's taking you through your own wilderness season. No matter what the path *looks like*, it is important that we **don't deviate from the path, despise the path, or despise the One who sent it.** Although the path is not always the prettiest or the easiest, it is what is needed to help us grow and to become who we were created to be.

Our charge as daughters of the Kingdom is to stay rooted in the path we've been placed on. Because when we remain, we allow God to work in us what we need for that season and the seasons to come. Also, if we allow God to finish the good work He began in us, we will be able to serve and lead others as well. We become better leaders when we soak in the process we're in. It is often the best training we will receive.

My best friend is a missionary in the Dominican Republic. She absolutely loves it. Prior to her leaving for the DR, she was involved in about six or seven different things. She was a Residential Assistant on her college campus, an intern at her school, an employee for a busy magazine company, along with several other things. This was her path, her assignment for that season. After graduation, the Lord uprooted her from school and moved her miles and miles away. Once she arrived in the DR, she immediately immersed herself in the culture and got to work. It was a very hard, but necessary season for her. I strongly believe that because she learned to be a chameleon in different environments in school, she was able to carry that same mindset into the Dominican Republic. She took a leap of faith and stayed on the path God had for her in school, until He called her to be somewhere else. And the best part about it is that she came into the next season *prepared* for it. Because God is constantly shifting us, it is important that we fully commit ourselves to the current path we are on. Whether you're in school, going after your degree, or believing God for that dream in your heart, stay rooted where He has you. God will *always* prepare us for the next path using the current one we're on, but it is up to us to fully surrender to the process.

Even when we face opposition and when we're being pruned, we must remain in the truth of God's word and we must remain on the path. I want to share four things that greatly encourage me to remain on the path.

1) *We must remember and trust the One who set us on the path.* Reflecting on the goodness of God will always be the fuel we need to continue on the path. It would have been in the Israelites' best interest to stop and reflect on the God who rescued them from slavery. But instead, their hearts were filled with murmuring, complaining, and unbelief (Exodus 1-10). Reflecting back on His faithfulness would have reminded them that they are with the God who split the Red Sea (Exodus 14), they are following the God who fed them and met their every need (Exodus 16:35), and they are under the protection of the God who heard their cry when they were in slavery (Exodus 3:9). How easy is it to forget His

faithfulness when we're in the midst of our journey? We must declutter our hearts from the filth negativity brings, by giving thanks and remembering His faithfulness. What has encouraged me over the years has been meditating on scriptures such as this one:

"Let all that I am praise the Lord; **may I never forget** *the good things he does for me. He forgives all my sins and heals all my diseases. He redeems me from death and crowns me with love and tender mercies. He fills my life with good things. My youth is renewed like the eagle's!"*
(Psalms 103:2-5 NLT)

When we're on our path and the cloud of doubt surrounds us, it's important that we pray these kinds of scriptures and let them be our *declarations*. Are you remembering the One who set you on your path? If not, you can begin by simply being thankful for all He's done. Give Him praise! Let's never forget the good things He has done for us, even when we're on a path we don't quite understand.

2) *We must learn to be flexible on the path.* One thing that I have learned about my journey with the Lord is that routes change. God is constantly guiding me in new directions, teaching me new things, and changing my course. Right after I graduated college, I moved in with my sister—this was not a part of *my plan.* Because I didn't have a full-time career yet, it was very difficult for me to get my own place, so staying with her was the best decision. Even though I could've moved in with my parents, I knew the Lord was leading me to stay with my sister, who I didn't have a strong relationship with at the time. I believe He wanted to heal some things within our relationship. Even though it got messy, that's exactly what He did. I'm so thankful for that season of my life because it is the season where I grew the most with God.

"If you try to hang on to your life, you will lose it. But if you give up your life for my sake, you will save it"
(Matthew 16:25 NLT).

To be flexible on the path means relinquishing control of the way we *think* our lives should be. We will journey down many paths with the Lord, but no matter which one we're on, we must remain *planted*. This means saying yes to God's way even when we want to go in the opposite direction. This also means doing things that are maybe a little out of our comfort zone. We can take heart knowing that no matter how many twists or turns we make, it will always lead us into the **good** plans He has for us.

"For I know the plans I have for you, says the Lord, they are plans for good and not for disaster, to give you a future and a hope" (Jeremiah 29:11 NLT).

3) *The path will always lead us Home.* The path will always lead us closer to the Lord. As I mentioned, the Lord designs unique, creative paths for us that will ultimately lead us into deeper intimacy with Him. After graduation, I worked a part-time job as a cashier, and during

that season I had a lot of free time. I believe this was one of the most pivotal seasons in my journey with the Lord. Not having a full-time job allowed me to explore God more, it allowed me to learn how to hear His voice, and even gave me the confidence I needed about my identity in Him. God used those job rejection letters to launch me into a greater knowledge of who He is. I'm so thankful!

I want to invite you daughters to seek the Lord in this season. No matter what you're facing, seek the Lord in prayer, in worship, and in the Word. *God desires for each one of us to be close.* I want to say that again, God wants to be close to YOU. We were never meant to live on our own. We're created to stay connected to the Father. So, sometimes He leads us on paths that will push us further into His loving arms. He desires for every daughter to not focus so much on the path itself, but on the One who created it. He's what matters the most. He wants us to know that He is our source. No matter who you are, trust that the One who sent you on this path will be faithful to complete what He has begun (Philippians 1:6).

4) *Preparation for the promise on the path.* I believe where many of us get stuck is by being frustrated in the place between our reality and our destiny. God has given us specific promises about our destination and we're anxious to get there. But God wastes nothing. So, you might feel like you're in the wilderness, but God is actually taking you on a path to prepare you for what's to come! Take your time and lean in to everything He's doing. God is in no hurry to rush us to our destination because He realizes that the preparation for the destination is more important than the destination itself. Why? He doesn't want us to be ill-prepared. God wants us to be successful when we arrive. Whether we have to go through a wilderness season like the Israelites did to transform their minds, or we practice a certain skill by going to school or taking a course—the Lord will always prepare and equip us for what He has called us to do.

If we look at the life of Noah, we see that Noah received a word from the Lord. Before the word manifested, Noah had to prepare. The Lord didn't just send the rain when half of the boat was done—no! He let Noah prepare for the rain before the rain came. It would have been foolish for Noah to stand around whining and crying about God not sending the rain when he wasn't even prepared for it to come.

This is what I believe God is saying to all of us today: you cannot ask God to send the rain if you're not willing to prepare for it. Just like the rain, God is eager to send out opportunities to use you, but it's up to you to prepare for it. It's important for you to prepare by praying and seeking the Lord with all of your heart, soul, and mind. I promise no matter what the journey looks like, if you lean in and obey, it will always lead you to the promises He has for you.

5) *We must be patient on the path.* I'll be honest, I have not mastered being patient. It is a fruit of the spirit that is still being worked on every single

day for me. However, I have been amazed by how much progress I have made by being planted on the *path* God has for me. I've seen this particular fruit grow the most, just by enduring through my seasons, especially the really hard ones. When I first moved to Atlanta, I expressed my interest in being a part of the worship team at my church. After I expressed my interest, I didn't hear back from the worship pastor for another four or five months. I honestly began to question my entire identity because I had not heard from them. I felt so defeated and wondered why God would call me all the way to Atlanta to join the worship team to just be rejected by them. Thankfully, because I allowed the Lord to develop patience in me during this time, I was able to see His plans for me unfold before my eyes. Was it a perfect process? No. But it was definitely something that I *learned*. No matter what path you're on right now, just be patient and allow God to perfect what He's doing *in* you and *for* you. It will always, always be worth it to wait.

Here's one final thought: The path will look different for each one of us, so don't get stuck on the side of the road comparing your life to anyone else's. Trust the One who's leading you, and cheerlead your sister along the way, too.

This is our hearts cry, this is our declaration: *"Father, if leading us through the desert is what you have for us, we will trust You enough to be right by our side. If we go high on the mountain top, we will not forget to obey You in all things. If You lead us into the valley to conceal us, we will trust that Your timing is perfect. And we will devote the path to knowing You more, loving You more, and becoming more and more like You. Heavenly Father, have Your way. This is Your life; do with it what You want to. Take us on the path You have for us."* In Jesus' name, Amen.

"...I remember how eager you were to please me as a young bride long ago, how you loved me and followed me even through the barren wilderness" (Jeremiah 2:2 NLT).

CHAPTER TWELVE:

By His Stripes

"But he was pierced for our rebellion, crushed for our sins. He was beaten so we could be made whole. He was whipped so we could be healed" (Isaiah 53:5 NLT).

God will take each of us on a path of healing. For so many years, I held onto the pain of my past. Because of the rejection, because of the fact that my dad wasn't emotionally there, and because I felt alone, I suffered in silence for many years. I suffered by choice. Even if people asked to help me along the way, I denied the obvious pain that was leaking from my heart. When I gave my life to Christ, I avoided surrendering my pain to the Lord even though deep down inside I wanted to know *why* I was hurting. Honestly, healing was way too scary for me. I was afraid to release the pain that became my home. I've learned that sometimes when you've been in a place of pain for so long, you create a home there because it's *comfortable* and *familiar.*

Remaining in that home for too long will acquaint you with neighbors around you that share your pain. Those neighbors could be bitterness, jealously, anger, resentment... the list goes on. I'll admit that I've met all of these neighbors.

I felt so at home in my pain that I eventually began to fight God on my healing process. He desired to heal me of everything I had ever faced, but I was too afraid of what it might cost me to let it go. So, I ran. I ran from the process of healing. I thought that if I gave Him my broken heart, He would keep me single forever. I thought if I gave up my nights of overeating, I would no longer have an outlet to distract me from the pain. I thought if I gave it all up and traded it to be with Him, it would take *too long* to process the pain I had been sweeping under the rug. Honestly, I'll be the first to say that avoiding healing affects everything in your life. It's better to just go through the process even if it hurts a little.

Can you relate to this? Maybe you find yourself in a place of pain, disappointment, or heartbreak. Have you ever thought about what it would look like to heal from the pain you've encountered? Maybe it would be deleting the photos in your phone of an ex. Maybe it would be forgiving someone who hurt you, as the Bible instructs us to do (Matthew 6:14). Or maybe it would take forgiving yourself for the mistakes you've made. I get it. It's scary to think about healing, but imagine the freedom that is attached to letting something or someone go. Imagine the weights that would be lifted off of you.

There's nothing that God can't heal—a broken heart, a family that's been torn apart from divorce, a woman who's been molested—nothing is impossible for Him. **God** is our healer. God knows our hearts. He knows our deepest pains and disappointments. With His love and power, He washes them away. This is what God desires to do with you. He wants you to see Him as a Father who heals, a Father who restores, and a Father who can make all things new.

Be okay with not being okay. The Lord taught me a very important lesson when I was healing and that's to be honest with myself, others, and most importantly, Him. He said to me one day, *"Jasmine, I want your honesty."* Understanding this truth led me into a freedom that I had never seen before in my quiet time with the Lord. Suddenly, I desperately wanted to unload *everything* onto Him and just cry out to Him. I encourage you to take *everything* with you into prayer and give it to the Lord. He can handle everything we bring Him, I promise you. Don't be afraid to pray about an area multiple times, ask Him for help…it's okay. It's okay to be sloppy and messy with God. He wants our cares. I think one of the biggest lies of the enemy is that we can't be real with God. But the Bible is clear when it says, *"Give all your worries and cares to the Lord, for He cares about you"* (1 Peter 5:7). Notice it didn't say *some* worries, it said *all* of them. Healing comes when we break down our walls and get honest before the Lord. It exposes the lies and the gunk in our hearts and allows God to gently wipe it away. He cares deeply about you; do you believe that? He knows and cares about all of those things you try and hide from other people and desires to heal every area.

There's a *safety* and *protection* in just being honest with Him. You can say things like, *"God, I need You today."* He hears those simple prayers. It is *okay* to be real with Him. After you get real, proclaim His truth over your life. This way, your prayers to the Lord are covered in the truth of God's Word. He will provide strength when you are honest about your weaknesses. He provides hope when you admit that you feel hopeless. And He provides everything that you need when you open yourself up and say, *I need You.* In this place, you are made whole in Him. Remember, He wants all of you—even your brokenness.

Surrender it to Jesus – I struggled greatly with surrendering the pain my ex caused me to the Lord. I distinctly remember wanting to get back with my ex, because to face the pain of being alone was just too much to bear. What I found was that when I didn't surrender, I wasn't moving closer to the Lord. I realized that the Lord would require nothing less than my everything. It reminds me of this verse: *"But Jesus told him, 'Anyone who puts a hand to the plow and then looks back is not fit for the Kingdom of God.'"* (Luke 9:62 NLT).

This verse led me to this thought: *Our healing is contingent upon our surrender.* If I surrender, I will find my healing. If you surrender, you will find your healing. So, I ask you, what do you need to surrender? Maybe it's lying, maybe it's cheating, maybe it's actually surrendering your trust to the Lord. Maybe it's that you need to completely trust that God knows how to change the person who hurt you and that it will be done in His timing, not yours. No matter what we're surrendering, we can rest assured that our surrender is never in vain. When we surrender to His will and His way, we will grow in wisdom, grow in His love, and grow in identity.

Another reason why it's so important to surrender is because we simply cannot heal by ourselves. The Lord wants to participate *with us* in the healing process. Often times, we try and find ways to heal on our own, but we usually end up making matters worse. We try to numb the pain by trying to go on vacation or maybe entering a new relationship, but none of these things can compare to the healing power of Jesus Christ.

Only Jesus can heal the deepest part of us. Only Jesus can restore us from the inside out. Only Jesus can take our pain and replace it with joy. You have to surrender the regret, the bitterness, the frustration, and the unforgiveness. I want to say this: if there's *anyone* you know that you have unforgiveness in your heart towards, I encourage you to forgive them as the Word tells us to do. This is a vital part of healing that can leave so much unnecessary pain on our hearts. Even if you never receive an apology, trust that God knows and is in control. Move forward in *your* healing, no matter what the past looked like (Mark 11:25).

The beautiful part about surrender is that we do not have to do it alone. He guides us in our surrender and searches out areas in our lives where we need to be freed. We just have to say yes. From there, He will meet us in our brokenness, pour in His healing power, and make us whole.

Even if you're still dealing with the residue of your past, believe that you are healed. Stop looking at your past and gaze upon the One who makes all things new. Don't be afraid to let go of the past. In fact, believe by faith that you are healed. You don't have to wait around to feel like you're healed. You can boldly declare it over yourself even if your emotions haven't caught up yet. In fact, every time there was a healing in the Bible, there was also an act of faith attached to it. When Jesus told the paralyzed man to walk in his healing in John chapter five, the man stood up in faith, believing he was healed. In the same way, we too can pick up our mat and walk.

I know it may seem impossible to live whole when you've spent your whole life in brokenness, but know this: *if Jesus walked in healing, we can too.* Jesus was lied to, cheated on, rejected, ignored, used, abused, went to the grave, and still chose to live in a place of wholeness with the Father. He chose to forgive, He chose to grace others, He chose to love them anyways, He chose to surrender His hurt to the Father, and He chose to not let the people's words affect the assignment God had Him on. Because He chose these things, we can choose them, as well. Speak healing over yourself, forgive who you need to forgive, and decide that you will not allow what has happened to you in the past hinder you from what God has for your future. We are healed, we are all healed in Jesus' name.

I believe that we will be the pioneers for our generation as we teach the world how to heal through the power of Jesus. I believe that, as we walk in healing, we will break generational chains that have been tied to many of our families. We will be the ones to show them how to love and how to grace others who hurt us. I believe that when we walk into this *boldly*, we will become exactly who we're called to be. We will change nations.

"He sent me to tell those who mourn that the time of the Lord's favor has come, and with it, the day of God's anger against their enemies. To all who mourn in Israel, he will give a crown of beauty for ashes, a joyous blessing instead of mourning, festive praise instead of despair. In their righteousness, they will be like great oaks that the Lord has planted for his own glory" (Jeremiah 61:2-3 NLT).

CHAPTER THIRTEEN:

The One

I remember the day I found out my ex was not the one. There was no peace within our courtship and things just fell apart piece by piece. I felt so deeply disappointed and didn't understand how I "missed God" on this one. He was saved and so was I, but it just wasn't God's will for us to be together. We had made arrangements to get married, even wedding planned a little before the ring (I wouldn't recommend this), and I really began to visualize my life with this man. It seemed as if it was a perfect fit. But after realizing that he wasn't the one, I began to sink deeper into the thought, "do I even know who I am without a man?" It took devastation and disappointment for me to realize that maybe my hope was in the wrong place. Maybe I actually needed a break from relationships to learn who I am in Christ and maybe I needed this time to know more about who God was, too. In this breakup, although my heart was broken into a million pieces, He was steering me back to the place I belonged.

Can you relate to this story? Maybe you've gotten your heart broken more than you're willing to admit and you just *know* there needs to be a change. I believe the biggest game-changer for Kingdom daughters is to realize who *the one* really is. The one that we long for, the one that we need is *Jesus*. He pursued us before we took our first breath. He is our source for everything we need. He is *the one*. No man, not even the kindest, finest Christian man, can ever fill our voids. When those longings are met by Jesus, we are able to see a godly man through the right lens. Do you desire a relationship/marriage? I challenge you to ask yourself, "why do I want a relationship?" Are your intentions to fill a God-sized gap in your heart? Are you lonely, maybe just wishing you had someone? Or maybe you're afraid that you won't get married and you want to be able to say you did it. I want you to know that God understands all your fears, your worries, and your why's—but more than anything, He wants to heal you. More than giving you someone, He wants to heal your heart from pain and rejection. It's from this place that we are made whole and are truly able to live in freedom with Christ.

The truth is, if you really want a deep, unconditional, safe type of love, you should pursue a relationship with Jesus Christ. You cannot find this type of love within anyone else. Even *believers* are flawed in showing His perfect love, so why not have the real thing in Jesus? I think the biggest lie we've believed is that *true love* is found in a man, but true love, *pure love*, perfect love, can only be found in our King. Jesus gave up convenience by walking with His cross, He gave up comfort by being nailed to it, and He gave up safety by being pierced on it. He did these things for *you*. This is the type of love you want in your life—one that sacrifices it all for love and intimacy. Do you understand that Christ died for you? He paid the price for your sins, even the sins you will make in the future, just so you wouldn't have to. Maybe this truth is hard for you to hold on to, but Jesus wants you to know how deep and how wide His love is for you (Ephesians 3:18). His love doesn't end, nor does it pull away when you change.

When we know that Jesus is the One that can satisfy us, we aren't so quick to jump into relationships. Because we know we belong to a

King, we no longer want to settle for less. There is a *confidence* that comes with knowing He is where we belong. Once I started to see that Jesus was and is my hope, I gave up looking for "the one." Not because I don't desire a husband, but because I realized that if everything I need is already in Him, I don't need to search anywhere else. He truly is enough. The more I grew in Him, the more I began to see that a lot of my desires for a man came from a place of loneliness and brokenness. I just wanted someone to love me and God confirmed that to me by saying this to me one night:

February 4, 2015: He said, *"Your loneliness is based on the fact that you've never really encountered Me in a way where you feel My presence and you are filled."*

I had to **learn** that Jesus was all I needed. The key word in this is *learn*. It reminds me of Paul when he said, "I am not saying this because I am in need, for I have learned to be content whether the circumstances. I know what it is to be in need, and I know what it is to have plenty. I have learned the secret of being content in any and every situation, whether well fed or hungry, whether living in plenty or in want. I can do all this through him who gives me strength" (Philippians 4:11-13 NIV).

This is the place that we have to get to—learning. We must be students of Christ. We must learn that Jesus is all we need. I think we lose sight of this truth and get frustrated when there's no man pursuing us, but what if this man that we've hoped for never shows up? Then where do we place our hope? Lord forbid anything happens to our future husbands, but what if the Lord calls them home? I've actually seen this happen to a Christian woman; her husband, the man she adored, died. And while I know the pain was and still may be unbearable, she carries such a light and a joy I know she only received from Jesus. Her joy inspired me. She held tightly to the hope and the grace of being known by God and is now fulfilling so much purpose in the Kingdom. Her hope is so wrapped up in Jesus that nothing could shake her, not even losing the man she loved.

What if our confidence was like that? What

if we dug our heels deep in the soil of wholeness in Christ and decided to not place our hope in anyone else? Man will always let us down and things come and go (Isaiah 40:8). He is steadfast and constant and He never changes (Malachi 3:6). We can rest in knowing that we are safe in Him. He is our anchor. He is our rock. Our hope in Him will never lead to disappointment (Psalm 62:6; Romans 5:5).

"Then they remembered those days of old when Moses led his people out of Egypt. They cried out, 'Where is the one who brought Israel through the sea, with Moses as their shepherd? Where is the one who sent his Holy Spirit to be among his people?'" (Isaiah 63:11 NLT)

CHAPTER FOURTEEN:

Surrender

I ran track for most of my life. I ran all throughout middle school and then stopped doing track after my freshman year of high school. I was a sprinter and I was actually *pretty good* at it. What I didn't know is that I would also be a runner once I got saved. Every time things would get hard, I would run away from God. I would push back prayer, I wouldn't study His Word, and I would pull away from church and community. In the first year of being saved, I didn't know how to surrender my emotions, hurt, and disappointment to the Lord. This led me to try and figure everything out on my own, which is a dangerous place to be in. Isolation usually leads to backsliding, loneliness, and unbelief. This is why community and fellowshipping amongst believers is so important (Hebrews 10:25).

There was a time in my life when I stopped trusting God regarding who I would marry. Like I mentioned in the previous chapter, I was once courting a man who I believed I was destined to marry. When we broke up, the disappointment of the relationship failing hurt so badly that I ended up trying to "heal" on my own. I journeyed down a road that I never thought I would take as a believer. I began to curse, I began to listen to rap music, I even drank a little bit. I couldn't contain how much it hurt to be apart from him. I just tried to find ways to numb the pain.

Even though we were broken up, we still wanted to remain "friends." **Huge** mistake. It was a mistake for several different reasons, *one* being that God told us to not be together, *two* because he was also running from God, and *three* because we both needed healing that we were running from. This led to us creating a bigger mess than there was originally. We kissed, we argued, we made up, and had all the relationship benefits without the title. Thankfully, we never had sex, but we definitely crossed all boundaries we had set. Before I knew it, I was making trips to see him even though God was telling me to cut things off completely. I tried to, but the thought of loneliness was too much to bear. I ended up at his place late one evening and I remember walking into his trashy, cluttered apartment. He had his beer out and some violent action movie on. I knew then that I shouldn't be there, but I just wanted to be with him.

It wasn't long before we got cozy. Things began to get heated and I began to drink. We began to spark up conversation that eventually led into one about us. I began to question him about his current relationship status. My emotions were heightened because of the alcohol and I ended up with his phone. On his phone, I noticed messages from girls all over the internet. I also saw text messages from a girl who I thought he had cut off. My heart sank. My buzz was fading away. I was furious. The crazy thing about it was that I discovered that he was texting his ex around the time we were courting. He was deceiving me when we were together. I was livid.

This moment was a turning point in my walk with God. I hit a dead end that I couldn't deny and the evidence couldn't be clearer that I needed to cut him off. In my stubbornness, God arrested my heart and gave me the strength to let it go. God wanted to protect me from more heartache and I could finally see that now. From that point on, I decided to make pursuing God my highest priority. I learned a valuable lesson after that: *just because you don't understand why you need to surrender doesn't mean that you don't need to surrender.* Whether you understand it or not, God has your best interest at heart. God began to take me on a journey of surrender when I ended that relationship. He began to press upon my heart to spend even more time with Him. I'll never forget when God spoke this to me:

December 2015: *"I'm not asking you to come into My presence when you feel like it. I'm asking you to come into My presence when you don't feel like it. That's when attacks come. Don't come home and try to relax. Come spend time with Me and let Me guide your next step; even down to watching videos. Declutter so that you can hear Me. So many have the calling, but very few have the discipline. Do not depart from the path I have called you to."*

I share this story because I recognize there are so many daughters who struggle with surrendering to the Lord. And my question to that is, why do we struggle so much? I believe it's because we don't know *who* we're surrendering to. When you don't know someone, you're hesitant to trust them, especially with your dreams, desires, and visions. When you know someone, and you know their heart for you, you can trust them fully without question. So, I want to journey around God's heart for a moment to share the importance of why He desires our surrender:

We must understand that we are nothing without the Lord. The Word says that it is in Him that we live, move, and have our being (Acts 17:28). There's nothing we can do in our own strength. This is why we surrender—to complete the union between us and God. Whether we are trying to live in a place of surrender, or trying to overcome sin, we cannot do it without the Lord's help. Invite Him into the areas you're weak in. He will be faithful to meet you where you are.

Surrender provides protection. I cannot explain to you how many times God has taken something away or closed a door to protect me. At the time, it didn't feel good, but eventually I would recognize why He closed that door. It is His heart to protect

His daughters, never to harm them. Can you imagine a father allowing his daughter to run on a dangerous highway? It would be negligent if the father didn't remove her from the highway, wouldn't it? It is the same with God. Because He's a good Father, He takes things away from us. We should be excited about surrendering to the Lord because He will always give us *His best* and protect us from danger.

"God is our refuge and strength, always ready to help in times of trouble" (Psalm 46:1 NLT).

Surrender is not accomplished by our emotions. I have made the mistake of allowing my emotions to lead my surrender, which was insincere. I even planned on going back to the very thing I was "surrendering." How many of you know that your emotions change? That is why it's important to surrender even those emotions to the Lord. When we are in a moment of surrender, God takes delight in a sincere, Spirit-led surrender. Just like the woman in Mark 12:44 who gave Jesus all she had,

He waits for us to surrender everything to Him, even our emotions.

Surrender positions us to receive His best—No matter what we're surrendering we can be assured that God will always position us for His best. Do you know that God wants you to have His best? Many fear that they won't receive the best if they surrender, but God does not withhold from us— especially when we surrender to Him. This does not mean that we surrender with ill-intentions of just wanting His best. We surrender because we love Him and want to obey His Word (John 14:15). Jesus promises that if we let go of our lives, we will discover what our lives are truly supposed to look like.

"If you try to hang on to your life, you will lose it. But if you give up your life for my sake, you will save it"
(Matthew 16:25 NLT).

Surrender helps to shift your perspective about your journey. It's easy to forget all that God has done for you, but when you're thankful, you will always remember that He is faithful. When you offer up praises to Him, you are choosing to thank Him for what He's already done. This provides the strength, the joy, and the faith to move forward into all He has planned for you.

Surrender allows us to be used for His glory. If I hadn't cut off that relationship, I wouldn't have been able to write this book. When you surrender fully to God, He will bring you into God-ordained opportunities that you could only dream of being a part of—but it always begins with surrender. When we surrender to Him, we are placed on a pedestal to shine brightly for His name's sake. This doesn't mean that you'll be placed on a stage, have a big following, etc. It could mean you show up to your job working in excellence; that's how you bring Him glory. It could look like starting a blog that He's been wanting you to create—that brings Him glory, too. When we surrender, we should always look to bring Him glory.

Surrender brings us Home. When we surrender everything to the King, we are able to move closer to the Lord. He wants all of you, even the parts of you that you feel you need to *"work on."* Being in His presence will allow us to be made whole, filled with joy and peace, and give us everything we need. Surrendering to the Lord is rejecting the broken cisterns that promise to fulfill and never do, and accepting Jesus who can and always will satisfy us.

This world is in desperate need of a Savior. We get to be the ambassadors that guide the lost Home. In a world filled with distractions, we are the ones who can show the world what they are searching for. Our surrender keeps us focused on the Great Commission; after all, that's what matters the most. He isn't asking for perfection, but what He is asking for is your *obedience.* God searches the Earth for daughters who will rise up and walk in obedience. Will you be one of them? Submit, surrender, and remove. There's someone on the other side of *your* obedience.

"Remember the things I have done in the past. For I alone am God! I am God, and there is none like me. Only I can tell you the future before it even happens. Everything I plan will come to pass, for I do whatever I wish" (Isaiah 46:10 NLT).

CHAPTER FIFTEEN:

Fighting Back

When we're on our journey home, we will run into Satan's attacks. Because you have been washed with the blood of Jesus, you are now in God's army, making *you* a target. This is good news because the war was already won 2,000 years ago by our Savior, but there are still real, daily battles we must face. Thankfully, God has given us everything we need to fight and we can arrive to battle fully-equipped and confident. If we haven't spent time preparing in prayer, reading, and meditating on the Word, we will lack confidence and the enemy will run us straight over. So, it is important that we understand *how* we fight and *why* we fight. I believe the women who will read this book are strong, courageous warriors on the inside; I desire to pull that warrior out of you.

When you're being attacked, you must acknowledge your identity in Christ. Who are you? Have you ever asked the Lord who you are? He calls you by name. He has numbered the very hairs on your head (Luke 12:7). You are unique, special, and important to God. I challenge you to take time out during your alone-time with God to ask Him about yourself. Ask Him these questions: *Do you have a specific name for me? Why did you choose me? What did you create me for? Who am I to you?* I also challenge you to search for scriptures that answer these questions. Anything that He reveals to you in prayer should be confirmed by scripture. The Lord loves to use His Word to speak to us.

When you're called into a spiritual battle, you **must** know who you are. Your identity will determine *how* you fight on the battlefield. If you grew up believing a lie about your identity, then that false identity will flow out of you. Maybe you grew up always being that safe, shy, reserved person; the enemy will latch on to any insecurities you may have from your childhood and take advantage of them. That is why the Lord wants to renew your identity even as a child, because your childhood, if left undealt with, will spill over into your adulthood. Not knowing your true identity as a daughter of God can truly hurt you or even hinder you from fulfilling all the plans God has for you. Not only that, but it will leave you feeling defeated about the battle when the enemy tries to attack.

There was a time in my life when God began to train me for battle in the quietness of His presence. When I asked Him *who I was to Him,* He began to tell me that I was His *warrior princess.* This took some time to get used to, but once I grasped what He meant by that, I took it and ran with it. I began to have this newfound confidence because I saw myself the way He sees me. I now see a brave, unstoppable warrior. So now, whenever I feel like the enemy is saying things to me like, "you're stupid," I fight back.

Do you know how God sees you? Have you ever asked Him how He sees you? Seeing yourself the way God sees you will change *everything* about how you fight in battle. It allows you to push aside the fear and anxiety, and look into the face of the enemy to declare "that's **not** who I am!" Because you know who you are, whenever the enemy comes to you and tries to tell you that you aren't a warrior, you aren't victorious, you are able to boldly declare with a roar, **"that's who I am!"**

Friend, I want you to be brave! I want you to be courageous! The truth is that it's a step-by-step process that the Spirit of God will take you on. I can only hope to show you different ways to equip you for the battle. It's as if you're a lion who believes you're a cat. There's a roar inside of you, but you've never once uttered it. You see other lions roar, but because you believe the lie that you're just a fearful cat, you let out a pathetic *meow*. Don't be afraid to be who God has called you to be. The longer you wait to roar, the more the enemy will tamper with your insecurities; he will convince you that all you can do is purr. I'm here to tell you that you already have the victory over the enemy. The truth is that you are a lioness who was born to roar! It's time to stop letting the enemy convince you otherwise. You are a fierce predator who has the power to overcome the enemy through the power of Christ! Are you ready to roar?

Coming into your Kingdom identity will push, stretch, and pull you out of your comfort zone. You're not doing it on your own. In fact, you're not the one fighting—it's the Holy Spirit within you. The Bible says, "the same spirit that raised Jesus from the dead lives within us" (Romans

8:11). Wow. Can you let that sink in for a second? The same Spirit that raised Jesus from the dead lives in us. He came out of that tomb, He defeated Hell, death and the grave—there is nothing impossible for Him, therefore there is nothing impossible for us! He lives within us every single day and He will faithfully show us our reflection as we read His Word. The Bible says the enemy prowls around looking for those whom He can devour—also known as the weak ones (1 Peter 5:8). So, consulting God in search of our identities works to our advantage; when we know our inherent power, we can rise up, roll our shoulders back, and know that there's nothing the enemy can throw at us that we can't catch and smash into the ground. The same Spirit that holds immeasurable power lives within each one of us. Know that the victory belongs to you. Because He conquered, you can conquer, too.

Meditate on these truths:

"I tell you the truth, anyone who believes in me will do the same works I have done, and even greater works, because I am going to be with the Father" (John 14:14 NLT).

"The Spirit of God, who raised Jesus from the dead, lives in you. And just as God raised Christ Jesus from the dead, he will give life to your mortal bodies by this same Spirit living within you" (Romans 8:11 NLT).

Three areas that the enemy tries to attack us in:

Unbelief – One of the ways the enemy tempted me with unbelief was by asking the questions, *"why should you serve God? Life isn't working out anyways."* I had to learn that sometimes when I will feel like quitting and giving up, it is the enemy trying to get me to doubt. Satan knows that when I believe, nothing can stop me. It's *so* important to turn worry into worship and strengthen your faith. When we have faith, even as small as a mustard seed, we can move mountains. The enemy would love nothing more than to lie to you so that you don't fight back. Unbelief hardens your heart toward God and renders you useless in battle.

"Today when you hear his voice, don't harden your heart as Israel did when they rebelled" (Hebrews 3:15 NLT).

I urge you: *don't* push God away when faced with fear. It will push you further and further into unbelief. You know how you sometimes hear about people falling away from faith? Well, most of the time it is caused by unbelief. That unbelief didn't begin by shouting, "I don't believe in God!" It was a quiet, gradual roll down into the valley of deception. But we will not be those who turn away from home; no, we will recognize where our faith is weakened and go after it to strengthen it. You are the brave one! You are more than a conqueror in Christ Jesus! You are victorious through Jesus! You are a daughter of the King! Drench yourself in worship daily and wear it as your perfume. The unbelief in your heart is nothing you can't overcome. I declare that over you today! Although you may see or feel unbelief, you do not have to entertain it. In fact, you can climb over it and keep running Home.

"We are pressed on every side by troubles, but we are not crushed. We are perplexed, but not driven to despair. We are hunted down, but never abandoned by God. We get knocked down, but we are not destroyed. Through suffering, our bodies continue to share in the death of Jesus so that the life of Jesus

may also be seen in our bodies" (2 Corinthians 4:8-10 NLT).

Procrastination—Maybe, like me, you have a hard time just *starting*. It could be writing a blog, or leading a project, and you just take forever to make a move. You think about all of your options before starting, and it's difficult to take that first step. There's so much anxiety that is tied to you even thinking about finishing it, so you never begin at all. I was recently watching an action movie. Within the movie, a woman was the main character and was a CIA officer. Prior to her being attacked, she would have to quickly pull out her best weapons to ensure she was safe. She was always a *few* steps ahead of her enemies. This is how we should be in spiritual battle. But unfortunately, so many of us wait to fight or maybe to not fight at all when the enemy attacks. By then, we're injured or too defeated to fight back at all.

We have got to stop worrying about the worst-case scenario and overthinking the spiritual battle that Jesus has already won. He shows us ways to fight that simply require our obedience. It's as if He's says, "I'm leaving you with my Word to speak and prophesy over your life." You do not have to allow the enemy to run you over any longer. Don't wait to fight when you feel strong, fight proactively knowing that your strength comes from the Lord.

"For I can do everything through Christ, who gives me strength" (Philippians 4:13 NLT).

Distractions—Our fight is always hindered and weakened by distractions. I believe that distractions hinder us from preparing for our next battle, and hinders us from fighting in our current battle. We prepare and fight with the Word, worship, and prayer, but if our focus is on something else, we'll be ill-prepared and empty. Distractions can be anything, from your phone, to social media, to people, to television, and more. When distractions arise, you can put up your shield and rise above them all victoriously.

There appears to be a battle between Christians and distractions in our generation. We're stuck between the choice we *should* make and the choice we actually make. We desire to become all that God wants us to be, yet we struggle to silence the distractions in our lives. I want to say this with all the love in my heart: you cannot overcome the attacks of the enemy if you're distracted! That means you can't walk through or overcome that problem in your life if you choose to submerge yourself in social media all day. The enemy will use your cell phone, that guy you know isn't right for you, or even your favorite video series to cause you to stumble, and ultimately get you off course. Ladies, I ask that you push the distractions out of the way and get back to a place of worship. You have to look past those distractions and start walking forward with your destination in mind. The enemy's plan is to leave obstacles of distraction in your path so that you'll never find your way back Home.

We must remember that the battle is not physical, it's spiritual (Ephesians 6:12). This means that the issue isn't your boss, your family, or even your friends—it's the spirit that operates behind them in order to distract you. I challenge you to ask the Holy Spirit what is distracting you from the fight. Then, I challenge you to cut whatever it is OFF. Distractions clutter our minds. In order to be who God has called us to be, we must have sober minds (1 Peter 5:8-9). If we are going to fight in battle, then we must first examine ourselves and make sure we don't have anything or anybody weighing us down. Strip off every weight ladies. Stand your ground and fight.

"Therefore, since we are surrounded by such a huge crowd of witnesses to the life of faith, let us strip off every weight that slows us down, especially the sin that so easily trips us up. And let us run with endurance the race God has set before us" (Hebrews 12:1 NLT).

Learning How to Fight

How do we fight? I've listed out a few ways that will help you in the battle. I pray that you lace up your shoes and start to use these truths to fight against your everyday battles.

Worship – We can kill the enemy's camp by simply using our voices in praise and worship. Our worship is powerful, and it carries a special place in God's heart—He loves it! There's proof that our worship is used as a weapon in 2 Chronicles 20, where King Jehoshaphat was faced with an army that would soon attack. The king was terrified but he immediately went into prayer seeking the Lord's guidance. Then, he ordered everyone to begin fasting. Then a powerful moment happens in verse 21, *"After consulting the people, the king appointed singers to walk ahead of the army, singing to the Lord and praising him for his holy splendor. This is what they sang: 'Give thanks to the Lord; his faithful love endures forever!"*

"At the very moment, they began to sing and give praise, the Lord caused the armies of Ammon, Moab, and Mount Seir to start fighting among themselves"
(2 Chronicles 20:22 NLT).

The opposing team killed themselves because the king and his army worshipped God! This exemplifies how our worship completely wipes out the enemy's camp. Your voice, not just your worship leader's voice, is a weapon. Don't be afraid to open up your mouth if you're afraid or faced with a situation that's bigger than you. God has already gone before you and fought for you—the battle is not yours. The Lord wants to participate with you in the battle (2 Chronicles 20:15). God will place worship songs on your heart that He wants you to sing out. When He does, don't be afraid to sing them. Just like the king and his tribe defeated an army with their voices, we can defeat the enemy with our voices, too.

The Word – There have been times in my life when I've tried to muster up the words to say when I felt attacked. For example, I would say, "I won't be afraid, I won't be afraid..." and say it over and over again. This isn't necessarily a bad thing, but it isn't the Word. Nothing can replace the Word of God. It is sharper than a two-edged sword. It will do more in twenty seconds than our own words can do in twenty years (Hebrews 4:12). We should learn from Jesus in Matthew chapter four when Jesus was led into the wilderness. Satan tried to attack Jesus three times and in three different ways, but each time Jesus remained consistent by fighting back with the Word. Here's an example:

"'...If you are the Son of God, tell these stones to become loaves of bread.' But Jesus told him, No! The Scripture say, 'People do not live by bread alone, but by every word that comes from the mouth of God'" (Matthew 4: 3-4 NLT).

During this time, Jesus was at the end of a forty-day fast, and the scripture says that He was *very hungry*. This tells me that the enemy will always attack you in your weakest moment and your weakest area, but even when he does, we have the privilege to use the Word to fight back. We must

197

mediate on the Word of God. This is how we equip ourselves and prepare. Joshua 1:8 says to study this book of instruction continually. It is our number-one weapon against the attacks of the enemy.

You can fight. You can do this. You will succeed. I don't care how long it's been since you've fought or if you're just now deciding to fight back; I want you to know that God is on your side. When we speak His Word in faith, it sounds like a dog whistle. A dog whistle emits sound that people can't hear, but animals can. It's the same with the Word of God. Maybe we don't hear the panic and fear the enemy's camp makes when we speak it, but to them, it's loud and clear. Don't hold back.

Prayer—Nehemiah knew what it looked like to pray to the Lord. Nehemiah was burdened to rebuild the wall of Jerusalem. But he had a need and knew that nothing would be accomplished without the Lord's help. So, he prayed to the Lord to help him. Here's a snippet of what he said:

"O Lord, please hear my prayer! Listen to the prayers of those of us who delight in honoring you. Please grant me success

today by making the king favorable to me. Put it on his heart to be kind to be" (Nehemiah 1:11 NLT).

Nehemiah had a need and instead of running to man, He sought God's face. He asked God to favor him before the king; in chapter two, we see that it worked. After Nehemiah prayed, the Lord gave him a plan of action. This is exactly how a spiritual battle works: first we pray to the Lord, then He shows us how to act. God is always faithful to give us a game plan for our fight. As we fight, the Lord will always pave the way to success.

What a blessing it is to pray to the Lord and confide in Him before we do anything! We must seek Him first because He knows best and will always devise the best strategy. God heard Nehemiah's prayers, and we can remain confident knowing that God hears our prayers, too. Rest assured that when the enemy attacks you, you are in the safe zone when you position yourself in prayer. With God, we always, always win.

"You will look in vain for those who tried to conquer you. Those who attack you will come to nothing. For I hold you by your right hand—I, the Lord your God. And I say to you, 'Don't be afraid. I am here to help you'"
(Isaiah 41:13-14 NLT).

CHAPTER SIXTEEN:

Sweet Wonder

Wonder: *a cause of astonishment or admiration*

I never knew I would be fascinated with airplanes until the Lord moved me close to the airport. As I would drive into work every day, I noticed these giant objects in the sky. I thought, "wow, this big airplane is able to sustain itself in the air." When you think about that, it's mind-blowing. Not only that, but while they are thousands of feet in the air, planes can also sustain the weight of the people riding inside of them. I found myself being excited to go into work each day just to see planes take off. It's the coolest thing to me, but to frequent fliers, planes probably underwhelm them because they're used to it. After seeing these planes, it sparked a thought in my mind: I wonder if we've gotten used to the things of God. Have the circumstances in our lives made us less excited about who He is? Do we still get excited about our testimonies and the faithfulness of God?

We should know something about God—He *loves* our wonder. He loves when our eyes light up with a scripture, He loves to see us get excited when we're in His presence, He loves to see us learning new things about prayer. He loves to see us explore His fullness. The Bible even teaches us that we should become like little children (Matthew 18:3). When I think of this verse, I think about living in a state of innocence and wonder. Just like a child would be excited to explore a new toy or see a new place, the Lord wants us always to be in a state of constant awe and wonder of Him.

I was talking to a sister in Christ one day, and we were talking about our journeys with the Lord. She said something to me that caught my attention.

"I remember I used to be so excited about spending time with God." Her statement troubled me and I wanted to get to the root of *why* she stopped spending time with Him.

So, I asked her, "What changed? What made you pull back?"

She responded with, "Just life…"

As she began to speak about all the things that she had faced, I began to think back to my journey and how at one point I, too, pulled away from the Lord. There was a time in my life when I was evicted from my apartment, when I had little to no money to buy groceries, and I felt like my relationship with God was failing. I quickly learned that whenever I placed my hope and security in my finances, or anything outside of God, my wonder drifted away.

I'm curious about what it would be like if we all stayed in a place of awe and wonder in our relationship with God. I wonder, what ministries would be birthed? What sermons would be taught? What songs we would sing? I wonder, if we took the time to study the life of Jesus, would we lack faith anymore? I wonder, if we understood the price that was paid on the cross, would we understand His love more? I wonder, if we fixed our gaze on things above and not earthly things, how much more would we share His goodness?

I think what hinders our wonder the most is when we meet face-to-face with hardship. We lose our trust in the Lord and we begin to doubt. David knew all about this place of uncertainty, but he also clung to God tightly so he wouldn't fall into the trap of complacency. In Psalm 57:8, David cried out for God to awaken his heart. David recognized that his heart may have hardened because of the tests and trails in his life. David knew that he needed God to breathe life into his heart during this time. Sometimes when you're in the midst of hardship, instead of pulling away from God, invite God into what you're going through like David did. Ask Him to soften your heart and to align you with what He's doing. God loves to help us in the midst of doubt, but He just wants our honesty first.

"For I cried out to him for help, praising him as I spoke. If I had not confessed the sin in my heart, the Lord would not have listened. But God did listen! He paid attention to my prayer. Praise God, who did not ignore my prayer or withdraw his unfailing love from me" (Psalm 66:17-22 NLT).

Are you still excited about God? Is your relationship with God in a state of awe and wonder? Are the things that God has spoken to you still ringing in your spirit? Are you learning something new about God that you are sharing with others?

By no means am I the perfect Christian. However, I do know what it's like to be complacent in my walk with the Lord. My hope is to bring you back Home with these truths. I want to save you from traveling down that path of complacency, or if you are in that place, I want to help you get out of it.

The Gospel—One of the reasons why we stray from Home and lose our wonder is because we treat the gospel like *it's just another story*. I'll be honest, this was me for a while. I didn't quite understand the gospel, so it made sense that I didn't get that excited about it like other people did. I want to encourage you if you find yourself in that place, to go a little deeper than you have before. Study the Word. Find out *how* the Gospel directly impacts you. Meditate on His love, the cross, and *the price that was paid for you*. These things will change your perspective and awaken your heart to the joy of salvation. The gospel is more than just a story. The gospel is everything. It is our reason for being. It is why we die to our flesh daily. It is why we surrender. It is our hope. It is our joy. When the gospel becomes mundane to us, that should scare us. There is nothing more important in life than the gospel.

Mankind was utterly lost in sin, and we deserved the wages of sin—death. The Father, in His love and mercy, sent His Son Jesus to die on the cross as payment for our sin. Because Jesus was the only perfect man, His blood was the only sacrifice strong enough to cover each and every one of us. He died the death that we should have died. But it didn't end there. Jesus rose from the grave and ascended into Heaven, proving to the world that He truly was God Almighty. This rescued us from the penalty of sin, eternal death, which gives those who accept Him eternal life! After His ascent, Jesus sent the Holy Spirit to live within each of us. He changes our course and guides us into a life of freedom! He died to free us from suicidal thoughts, He came to free us from loneliness, and He came to redeem us from heartbreak. He set us free!

The gospel is not just another story; it is the truth about life, death, and true love. Our eternity rests upon it. If your heart has been hardened to the gospel, I urge you to surround yourself with people who can help you to reignite your passion. I also urge you to pray. Pray that God would stir your heart up once more to the joy of the gospel. Our wonder of the gospel changes everything in our walk with the Lord—everything.

The Tests and The Trials—I believe what is discouraging daughters from pursuing a lifestyle of wonder the most is the tests and the trails of life. They come into our lives and they try to steal away our fascination with God. I've been there: lifting up my hands in service, feeling overlooked and forgotten about by the One my lips sang about. It's a lonely place. I've learned that when I am absorbed with the storm around me, I am less likely to fix my eyes on who He is. This then leads to me to questioning if this journey with Him is even worth it. If I'm not careful, this leads to wanting to quit. But when I am absorbed in His Word about who He is (not what I am not) and I am memorizing scripture, my storm seems like a puddle of water.

So, if you find yourself in the midst of a storm right now, I would encourage you to not spend all your time trying to fix the issue in front of you. Instead, meditate on the truth of who God is, spend more time in prayer, and surround yourself with a community hungry for God. Don't grow weary when you don't understand. Reach out for help instead. He will bring books, sermons, and people across your path to encourage you. It's so worth it to push through difficult times. You don't have to do it alone. Learn about His nature in this season, *find a new reason to praise* Him—there's always a new reason. This will be your fuel, your joy, and your strength to get you through. Don't allow a *temporary* season to steal your worship of our King— He is and always will be faithful.

Daughters, our wonder will be the very thing that will draw in unbelievers and it will be the very thing that keeps us in the race. Choose to worship. Choose to praise. Even in the dry seasons, even in the mountain top seasons, seek Him with your whole heart. Let's be daughters who choose to be rooted in an awe of our great God and draw others to Him through our worship.

"And I will make an everlasting covenant with them: I will never stop doing good for them. I will put a desire in their hearts to worship me, and they will never leave me. I will find joy doing good for them and will faithfully and wholeheartedly replant them in this land" (Jeremiah 32:40-41 NLT).

CHAPTER SEVENTEEN:

For Such a Time as This

"And who knows but that you have come to your royal position for such a time as this?" (Esther 4:14 **NIV**)

When our hearts are full of awe and wonder of God, we can carry the Father's heart everywhere we go and ignite a fire within people we meet every single day. No matter what season you might find yourself in, it's important that you know that you have been called for such a time as this. I want to lay out five final principles that you can take with you as you fulfill the calling of God on your life. God is not waiting to use you later on. He wants to show you how He can use you right where you are. Even if you're not on a stage, your entire life is a stage that the world is looking at. Share the light that you've been given. We were never meant to dim it; shine it for the world to see.

Oftentimes, the most impactful callings require the most isolation. I want to be really honest with you. When I was writing this book, the Lord kept me hidden. There weren't many outings with friends, vacations, family time, or socializing. Instead, I stayed up late, woke up at 5 a.m., went straight to coffee shops

212

after work, and even worked on this book in random parking lots. I was praying over those who would read it more than talking on the phone and using my lunch breaks to cry out to the Lord for strength. Writing a book is no joke. I had to persevere through the isolation. But through the isolation, the Lord met with me. He showed me things in the secret place that I probably wouldn't have seen any other way. I want you to know that the road to your calling may be lonely, but there is always a community of other believers who are going through the same thing. It's normal. It's going to be okay. Keep yourself hidden in His presence, the reward and fruit you will bear will be great!

Your calling will not look like anyone else's. The Lord has uniquely designed your calling for *you* to enjoy. What would happen if every Christian was a pastor? Everyone would be on stage and no one would be tending to the children, leading worship, or helping run the service. Not one believer's purpose is more important than the other; we all count (1 Corinthians 12:14-26). So as the Lord calls you in where you're supposed to be, do *not* compare. When we compare, it only leads to us overthinking and assuming our roles don't matter. You matter. We are one body, working towards the same goal, and we all need each other—no matter what role you have. Let's get back to trusting God with our journeys and celebrating each other along the way.

Your calling will flow out of your intimacy with Jesus. You might think you need to follow a certain formula in order to walk out your calling. The truth is, the Lord never created us to follow formulas; He created us to follow His spirit. From His presence, the Lord will lead and guide you into the places you are supposed to go and the people you are to meet. I didn't know that I was called to lead worship until the Lord showed me in the secret place. Not only did He show me, but He also told me the steps to take to pursue it. His plans for you will flow out of the time you spend with Him. That is the place Jesus wants us to lead from—true intimacy. There are many things we can do to become a speaker, publish a blog, create a business—but the first place we should begin is His presence. Hustle will never produce Kingdom purpose, but seeking the Lord will.

The Lord never created us to follow formulas; He created us to follow His Spirit.

We must say what the Lord says, and we must do what the Lord does. God will always call us out of our comfortable places to set us on high places we've never seen before. Sometimes I wonder where I would be if I hadn't moved to Atlanta. I probably wouldn't be writing this book, blogging, or leading worship. Sometimes, it scares me to think of what would have happened if I hadn't moved. What we grow to become has everything to do with our environment. If we're surrounded by chaos and dysfunction, we will bear the fruit of chaos and dysfunction. If you're considering changing your environment, then pray, pray, pray. Make sure that as you move, you're led by the Spirit of God.

Everyone moves and transitions in their own seasons and in God's perfect timing; however, you must lean in and listen to where He wants to place you. Your heart must be guarded from family members, friends, and loved ones. If they are not Spirit-led, they can pollute the message that God is speaking to you. You must go when He says go. If He says write a book, you write. If God says go be a graphic designer, you become a graphic designer. You fix your eyes on one place for approval—Jesus Christ.

For years, I became a slave to my dad's approval. I wore his disapproval like an open wound. I grew up working so hard to be noticed by my dad. I knew with me moving to Atlanta, it would pull me out of bondage to my dad's approval. So, when it came time to move, I chose what the Lord said over my dad. He said move, and I moved. Within a week, I packed up my room, filled my car with boxes, and left the following week without any concrete plans. It happened so quickly, but I believe it needed to happen that way. I needed to prove to the Lord I would be obedient to Him even if it caused questions and doubts on my dad's end. Sometimes when we're fulfilling the calling on our lives, we have to say "yes" to God and "no" to man—even our own family.

"Obviously, I'm not going to win the approval of people, but of God. If pleasing people were my goal, I would not be Christ's servant" (Galatians 1:10 NLT).

My question to you is, will you be Christ's servant, or will you be a slave to people?

In a world filled with darkness, you carry the light that the world needs to see. It's time to shine. This is the time to become exactly who you've been created to be. There is so much hurt, chaos, and confusion happening right now in the world and they need to see Jesus in us. Do we dare cover the light that drew us out of the darkness? Who covers a burning light, especially if that light will lead others home? I often use this example when encouraging other women. I ask them, "if the person who led you to know God decided not to post that caption or preach that sermon or tell you God loves you, where would you be?" It's important that we recognize that we carry that same gift and we can walk in the same authority as they did to bring others to the Lord.

"No one lights a lamp and then covers it with a bowl or hides it under a bed. A lamp is placed on a stand, where its light can be seen by all who enter the house" (Luke 8:16 NLT).

This verse makes me think of a lighthouse. Lighthouses are usually used as a navigational aid and used to warn boats of storms and danger. We are the lighthouses for the Kingdom and we shine bright for all the world to see. When the storms of life are raging, we are the ones firmly-planted to show people the way Home. When others give up, we pull them up and tell them to keep going. When others lose their way, we are able to guide them back to the loving Father.

No matter where you may find yourself in this season, know that there is something God wants to do in and through you right where you are. Maybe it's ministering to your coworkers, maybe it's joining a small group, maybe it's starting a movement. Regardless of what it is, do it with bravery and with fearlessness knowing that God is on your side. Let's be world-changers for the Kingdom of God and walk in our God-given destiny.

"Then this city will bring me joy, glory and honor before all the nations of the earth! The people of the world will see all the good I do for my people, and they will tremble with awe at the peace and prosperity I provide for them"
(Jeremiah 33:9 NLT).

CHAPTER EIGHTEEN:

The Return

I ran from the Lord after I gave my life to Christ. I feared surrendering to His will and giving up mine. I knew when the Lord placed this book on my heart, He wanted me to share that journey with you. Why? Because the truth is, many of us within the body of Christ have left Home. It may be out of frustration of the season we're in, or doubt and worry have overtaken our lives. No matter what the reason is, my heart's cry for each one of you reading this is that you'd never lose sight of the One you serve. At times, we may grow weary, feel stuck, or even be tempted to give up. But it's in those moments when we have to dig deep into the truth of God's Word to continue the race before us.

Guys, I wish I could tell you that there won't ever be moments in your journey when you won't want to leave Home. I wish I could tell you that there won't be any storms raging in your life. I can't. But be encouraged that God promises to work all things together for your good (Romans 8:28). When your strength is low, you can find it from continually seeking His presence, even when you're at your lowest (Psalm 105:4). There have been many, many times when I've wanted to quit this journey, but a sister was there to encourage me to endure. As *your* sister in Christ, I'm telling you: you can't quit! Get into His presence and you will find strength to keep running the race!

Each one of you carries something special that the world is waiting to see. You carry gifts and talents that were hand-crafted by your Heavenly Father. How cool is that? He desires to use those gifts to further build His Kingdom *and* to give you fulfillment of living a life of purpose. He wants to shine through you as you work your nine-to-five, while you stay on your college campus, as you live amongst your family, and so much more. Many of us believe the lie that we can only live a life of purpose if we're on a stage, but that's not true. As long as you are a consistent, willing vessel and remaining in His presence, there will always be a new ministry opportunity for you. You just have to see your life through His eyes and not your own. He wants to do great and mighty things through you and in you right where you are!

It's in His presence that our ministries, our callings, our gifts, and our talents will be birthed. It's not on a stage, or working for the largest ministry. It's by creating a life of intimacy with the Father. It all begins at Home. When we sit at the Father's feet, He will show us which way to go, how to depend on Him, and how to live a life full of purpose. There's nothing we can birth in our own strength that will last, but everything that will last will come from pursuing His presence (Zechariah 4:6).

I believe the Lord is saying to you: steward your time with Him well. That means no more excuses. Get back to prayer, worship, and meeting with Him daily. This is the heartbeat of this book. I believe He is telling us to tear down the walls of distraction and come and sit at His feet. Whatever that time with Him looks like for you, He wants you to remain in that place. Not because it's a law, but because you love Him and want to live a life fully devoted to Him. When we got saved, God promised to make a home within us. He would place His Spirit within us so that we'd never have to live apart from Him (John 14:16). As we abide in Him, as we let His Spirit lead us, we will begin to bear fruit that the world will be amazed to see. I believe we will begin to see miracles and wonders; I believe we will be the generation that will capture the very heart of God and showcase it for all the world to see.

Now more than ever is the time to rise up and become the daughters we're called to be. To become those daughters, we must plant ourselves in His presence. We are called to show this broken world how to pursue the presence of God—let's show them! We've discussed many ways that we can get off-course from pursuing the Father, but I encourage you to examine your own life to see what areas are holding you back. Rid yourself of the roadblocks and as Jeremiah 31:21 says, *"...mark well the path, by which you came. Come back again, my virgin Israel; return to your towns here."* Come back to the Father. No matter how long it's been, no matter how weary you are, no matter how much brokenness you carry, you are always welcome Home.

Notes

Chapter Three: *Intimacy* -

http://www.dictionary.com/browse/intimacy

Chapter Four: *Cisterns* -

https://en.wikipedia.org/wiki/Cistern

Chapter Five: *Vain - biblehub.com*

http://biblehub.com/topical/v/vain.htm

Chapter Fifteen: *Dog Whistle* -

https://en.wikipedia.org/wiki/Dog_whistle

Chapter Sixteen: *Wonder* -

https://www.merriam-webster.com/dictionary/wonder

Chapter Seventeen: *Offense*

https://www.google.com/search

Chapter Seventeen: *Sovereignty* -

http://www.christianity.com/theology/what-does-the-phrase-god-is-sovereign-really-mean-11555729.html

Chapter Seventeen: *Lighthouse* -

http://www.dictionary.com/browse/lighthouse

Printed in Great Britain
by Amazon